LESSONS *for* JOEY

LESSONS *for* JOEY

100 Things I Can't
Wait to Teach My Son

[signature]

RJ LICATA

Lessons
and
Love

LESSONS & LOVE PUBLISHING
SYRACUSE, NY

Lessons & Love
PO Box 182
Kirkville, NY 13082
www.LessonsandLove.com

Ordering Information:
Quantity sales. Special discounts are available on quantity purchases by corporations, associations, and other groups. For details, contact the publisher at the address above or through the contact form on the publisher's website.

Edited by:
Tison Kelley
Doreen Miori-Merola
Nancy Pasquale
Danielle Kosecki

Photo credits:
Lesson #96 by Veronica Pagano
Lesson #74 by Kelly Bennett
Lesson #24 by Sharlotte Salamon

Back cover photo by Kevin DeMassio: www.kevindemassio.com

To Mom & Dad,
for teaching me love,

and Dani,
for giving me the greatest gifts of all...

ACKNOWLEDGEMENTS

Writing this book was a labor of love, for sure, but it would never have had a chance were it not for the help of some wonderful people…

A big thank you is due to everyone who afforded me their time and expertise—especially the very talented Tison Kelley, Doreen Miori-Merola, Nancy Pasquale, and Danielle Kosecki, for their sharp eyes and attention to detail during the editing process. Their guidance has proven invaluable.

I'd also like to thank my very good friend Kevin DeMassio, of Kevin DeMassio Photography, whose photography skills make me look much better in headshots than I do in real life. Special thanks also to Veronica Pagano (#96), Kelly Bennett (#74), and Sharlotte Salamon (#24) for permission to use their photographs in my lessons.

I am grateful to everyone who offered encouragement on Facebook. Your initial support jumpstarted this project, and your continued support has provided the inspiration necessary to complete it. This includes all my friends who've agreed to help spread the word now that the book is finished.

Thanks to Tim Ahern, an associate-turned-mentor and now friend, for his continued guidance and encouragement. We all need someone outside our family who's not afraid to force us to take an honest look at ourselves, and address the pieces that need to be addressed. Tim has done all that and more for me. I only hope one day I can help someone else the way he's helped me.

To my buddies, who made dramatic impacts on my life and left imprints on my soul: Without time spent with you all, I wouldn't know what to warn Joey about. Still, some of my favorite conversations begin with the words, "Remember that time when…"

My family—immediate, extended and in-law—have always shown me nothing but love and support, regardless of what I was working on, and the evolution of this project was no different. Things like this tend to consume my thoughts, and I'm sure I wore some of them down with my obsession. Still, they listened to every idea I had, every story I told, and every dream I dreamt. Most importantly, they encouraged me to make them all real.

Throughout my entire life, my brother, Mike, has been a trusted friend and partner in imagination. I have long been able to count on him for whatever I needed, whether it was a dose of reality or something to make me laugh. His insight into the subject matter of this book has been extraordinary.

To Mom and Dad, the original authors of all these lessons, I am so fortunate to have you as my parents. Now, having gotten my own taste of parenting, all I can do is say 'thank you…for *everything*.'

Finally, to the three people who inspire me daily to be the best person I can be, who've shown me the true definition of unconditional love, and who are the cause of so much joy in my life: my beautiful wife Dani, and our wonderful children, Joey and Gianna—I love you all. Thanks for being so awesome.

FOREWORD

RJ Licata has done something brilliant. As with many such ideas, you're apt to ask yourself, "Why didn't I think of that?" I know I did.

If you're reading this, you, like me, and RJ have discovered the great and obvious secret to happiness and success in *this* life: It's about having close relationships with people who we'd die for. That's what I tell students as I travel the country speaking about the significance of education and character and the importance of reading to strengthen us in both. I contemplate what it means to be a success, then surprise them by saying it has nothing to do with being an eight year veteran in the NFL, appearing on television, or being a bestselling author. I tell them that success is being a good mother, sister, partner, friend, brother, son, or FATHER.

Being a father is what this book is about, fatherhood, and even more specifically, being father to a SON. Since I have two daughters I love infinitely, I'm not uncomfortable saying that my whole young adult life I dreamed of having a SON. For a man, there's something about it I don't feel we have to explain or justify. It's the way it is, and the way it's supposed to be. Like all great gifts, though, to truly appreciate it, we need to step outside our everyday routine, stop, think, reflect, and savor the great gift of a son. RJ has given us a manual on how to do just that.

Our quest for immortality is partially assuaged by having a son. They are us, continuing on into the future... forever? Maybe, and we want them to be the best they can be... certainly better than we are. To do that, we need to teach them the important things *in a life* where so many others will spend time and money trying to convince them that success is a big house, a fancy car, or people asking for your autograph. This book does that, teaching our sons and reminding us what really matters, things like love and loyalty and perseverance, integrity and creativity.

As you read this book you will be reminded of your own 100 things you need to teach your son. Some of them will be exactly the same as RJ's, some you will make up on your own. Those of us lucky enough to have found this powerful book will make its precepts a part of our lives and a part of our greatest quest: fatherhood.

Enjoy.

Tim Green
April 2014

Give a man a fish and you feed him for a day.
Teach a man to fish and you feed him for a lifetime.

- Chinese Proverb

INTRODUCTION

When my son was first born, I was eager to begin being his dad. I knew there were many things I wanted to teach him and many experiences I wanted to share. Of course, there's not much you can teach a newborn other than love. So that's where we started. I set aside the more complicated parts of life for a time when he'd be better able to understand them, and focused instead on just loving the little guy up. I think most parents will agree that part is pretty easy. But just because it's easy doesn't mean it's not important. If you want even a fighting chance at teaching the other stuff, you've really got to show that you love them, first and foremost. Don't you think?

During the next two years, I didn't think much about my big plans for teaching Joey about life until, one day, it suddenly occurred to me that not only was he ready, but that the learning had already begun. It seemed like one minute he was an adorable mass of involuntary movement, helplessly leaking from all orifices, and the next he was ruling our household with an iron fist. Somewhere along the way he'd absorbed plenty of what was going on around him, and I remember talking with my wife about how we were entering a period where we were no longer only caregivers—the parenting had begun. The things we did and said—to him and to each other—would mold him into the person he'd become. It was time to ask ourselves what we valued most, and what it would take to instill those values in our little boy.

One afternoon, on a whim, I made a post to my Facebook profile, announcing one of the things I couldn't wait to teach my son. Without any real intentions of formality, I randomly labeled it #100, added a photo that helped to explain it visually, and hit 'post'. I didn't necessarily plan to continue the list, and certainly never expected to count all the way down to #1. To be honest, I kind of forgot about it until a few days later when another lesson popped into my head. I posted that too, and before i knew it, my friends were liking, commenting, and asking for more. From there, I felt I had no choice but to continue. So every morning, for the next ninety-eight days, I posted a new lesson and photo. I knew I was putting together something that Joey would eventually appreciate, but without the positive feedback from others, it probably would have begun and ended there. As I got closer to finishing the list, it occurred to me that people beyond my circle of friends might also enjoy these lessons, so I created a Facebook page devoted strictly to this idea. When that took off, I knew I couldn't stop. And not long after, I began writing this book.

This project has been both the most rewarding and the most difficult thing I've ever done. It wasn't the actual writing that was hard as much as the finality of the words. I often thought: *Is this really how I want to address this topic? Could I have said it better?* Yes, we parents think those things on a daily basis, but the difference here was I hoped my children would reference the lessons as they grew up, and maybe even pass them on to their own children. What I wrote needed to be what I truly felt. I created a lot of pressure for myself that way.

Another thing that I think about often is how writing this book might create pressure for my kids. Will they have to live up to a standard I created for them? Maybe. It might be challenging, but it's not all bad. Still, for those who feel inclined to expect them to be perfect just because their dad wrote a book, I encourage you to read Lesson #85. And #73. And #71. They aren't perfect. And neither am I. Aside from the joy of having something so personal to pass on to my children, the greatest reward I received from writing this was the opportunity to learn about myself. I can't tell you how many times I would write a lesson and think: *Wow, that's pretty good, but I had NO IDEA I felt that way.* I learned things I believe in and things I need to work on, too. It's important to note that I didn't write this thinking of myself as someone who has it all figured out. I have room to improve on each of these lessons as well.

Despite my concerns, I had many good reasons for writing this book. I wrote it for those who encouraged the list on Facebook, reassuring me that there really was some value in it. I wrote it for those who are reading it now, and for all those who will ever read it, to remind us all that we are each choosing our path every day—in the way we think, and in the things we do, and in our general approach to life. I wrote it in hopes that it might offer someone, somewhere the inspiration they need to say the things to their own children that they had once struggled to find the words to say. I wrote it as a reminder that creativity is nourishment for the soul, and that there is always room for more.

More than any other reason, I wrote this book for my kids. I wrote it so that, despite any physical distance between us, they will never feel like I'm too far away. I wrote it so that they'll always have my advice ready for the taking. Of course, whether or not they actually do is another story. I believe that our children need what's in our hearts much, much more than they need what's in our wallets. This book is my attempt at giving them what's in my heart. And what I have in my heart for them is love—overwhelming, unconditional love. See, even once they're old enough to understand everything you want to teach them, it still seems to come back to that one thing, the thing they've always understood, since the moment they were born: love.

RJ Licata
Syracuse, NY

#100

Even when you feel small and insignificant, there's still something big and great inside you.

Greatness lives within you. It lives within all of us. Sometimes it's easy to forget that, though. It's easy to feel lost in a world that moves so quickly and is so darn big. Life has a way of beating us up and kicking us while we're down. It can be demanding and relentless and unforgiving. It can make us feel as if we are unable to make a change, like there's no way we could make a difference in a world as vast and unsympathetic as ours. But that's simply not true. The truth is, even when you feel small and insignificant, there's still something big and great inside you. It's always there. And it's just waiting for your permission to come out. So let it out. Let it show how great you can be.

As our own biggest critics, we tend to dwell on the times we come up short; we remember our failures, often letting them overshadow our successes. Sometimes we need a reminder that we are much better than our worst moments. We need to realize we're capable of even *more* than our best successes. There are no limits to our potential, except for the ones we place on ourselves. Others may try to slow us down, and our shortcomings may cause doubt, but if we can figure out a way to ignore them—to *overcome* them—we'll start to see some of that greatness come to life. We'll begin to believe that it's there, and we'll learn how to call it out again and again. And once you get that snowball rolling, it's tough for *anyone* to slow it down.

The definition of greatness is different for everyone. It could come from a lifetime of work or a single moment of heroics. It can be widely known or fly completely under the radar, but it often lends itself to helping others in a way that no one else can, or to improving things in a way that didn't exist before you came along. It comes by bringing something to the table that only you can bring and offering it to anyone who stands to gain from it. It occurs when you leave a lasting impact on the lives you touch, so that others are better for having known you. You always have this capacity for greatness, no matter what your day dumps on you, but you have to be willing to pull that potential out from the rubble that it might be buried under. You have to be aware that it's needed and be ready to unleash it. You have to *know* that you are able.

Discovering ourselves is a process. Every day we're growing and learning and improving, in hopes that we'll be better than the day before. No one has all the answers. None of us does everything as well as we'd like. But those who make progress do so because they trust their potential, and they refuse to let their past struggles define them. One mistake does not define your character. One failure does not define your ability. But one belief could define your potential. It's up to you to choose which beliefs you will listen to and which direction you will go. It's *your* responsibility to seek the greatness that is within you and to trust it, even in your weakest moments. The times you feel the smallest are when you need to believe the most. Let it come out. Don't be afraid to be great.

#99

Loyalty is lost. Stand by your team.

Everybody loves a winner. I get it. It's why we watch sports in the first place. It's the general motivation behind any competition. Still, there's something to be said for loyalty—especially when the team, group, or individual is having a difficult stretch. Sometimes they make it easy for you to want to bail on them and go sit down with the people who have something to cheer about. I've been there. I've lived it. But I try not to give in to the temptation, and I don't want you to, either. Be patient and have some faith.

One day that floundering team or struggling athlete—the one that you love and want to see do well—will start to win. They will get in a groove, things will begin to click, and they'll win some more. They will begin to climb out of the basement—no longer causing you to hang your head in shame and threaten to bail in frustration. They may not become champions. They may not even stay out of the basement for very long, but one day they'll have their shining moment, and they'll give their loyal fans something to cheer about. They'll give you a reason to be proud. *If you're still there.* And if you're still there, you'll not only feel the excitement of their most recent moment of glory, you'll also feel the relief of all the frustrating moments that threatened to pull you away. Most importantly, you'll feel the pride that comes from believing in something when few others did. You'll be one of the few who saw a bright spot in so many dark days. It's true when it comes to cheering on your favorite teams. And it's true with people, too.

Your friends, your family, those closest to you—if you know them long enough, they will all do something to let you down, myself included. They may not intend to do it. They may not even know they're doing it, but it's pretty much guaranteed that they will disappoint you at one time or another. Some of these disappointments will be more painful than others. But if you love those people enough, if they're your "team", then you owe them a fair chance to get out of the "basement." Let them show you that you were right to believe in them in the past, and that there's still good reason to believe in them now, even after they've done wrong.

It's not always easy. It's rarely fun. But when the day comes that they finally get it together, and they take that step outside the basement, you'll see that it was worth it. And when they put a few more steps together and walk out into the sun, you'll be proud—both of them and of yourself. It doesn't take a special kind of person to see the good in someone when they are flying high for all to see, but it takes a *very* special kind of person to sit down next to someone in the dumps and stay with him until he finds a way out. It's a sad truth that loyalty is lost in many ways. Don't contribute to the loss. Stand by your team.

#98

Popcorn and a movie with Dad beats getting in trouble any day.

You're not always going to want to hang out with your mom and me. At some point, you'll prefer to spend that time with your friends. That's okay. I get it. It's normal. It's also normal that you'll enjoy our company again one day, most likely once you've realized that we were never out to make your life miserable or give you a hard time. You'll understand that it was actually the opposite, and everything we did was about trying to make your life better and more enjoyable. As your parents, we are charged with teaching you responsibility and discipline, and to do so in a way that offers you even more opportunities than we had growing up. That's the idea, anyway. But in order for us to do our jobs effectively, you have to help us help you. It starts with making smart decisions.

We all know the difference between right and wrong. When we do wrong it's often because we give in to temptation or choose to ignore our conscience. The benefits are usually temporary and the cost is typically much more than we expected to pay. In short, it's *not worth it*. Still, we allow ourselves to be so consumed by status, appearance and reputation that our judgment becomes clouded. We don't think rationally, and we don't consider the future. We're looking for instant gratification, and we'll worry about the consequences later. Well, when the debt is due, we quickly realize just how short-sighted our decisions were. We may wish we hadn't been so impulsive, but by then it's too late. All we can do is hope we can recover from our mistake.

The best thing you can learn to do is recognize when trouble is near and remove yourself as quickly as possible. Do your best to avoid those dangerous situations. Sometimes this involves saying "no" to hanging out with a certain crowd or to attending a party. It requires you to sacrifice something you may want to do in the short-term, so that you'll be able to do more important things later on. It might cost you "friends", it might "damage" your reputation, and you could "miss out" on the party of the century, but if that's what it takes to keep you out of trouble, or to keep you alive and well, or to get a step ahead of the competition, then it's the only decision there is. Trust your instincts, listen to your gut and always choose right over wrong, no matter how tempting it is to do otherwise.

For a young person, all of this can be very challenging. It's hard to be a kid. There are pressures thrown at you from all different directions and expectations are often unfair. Their weight can become overwhelming. Sometimes the difference between right and wrong isn't as black and white through your eyes as it is through those of a more experienced, impartial adult. I can appreciate that dilemma. I can sympathize with your difficulty trying to make everyone happy and still keep your head above water in the process. I was there once myself. And it wasn't as long ago as you might think. I haven't forgotten the challenges you face. Which is why I'm happy to be there to help you through them. Maybe it's a heart to heart talk. Maybe it's an unspoken nod of encouragement. Maybe it's popcorn and a movie. Whatever it is you need, I'm here.

#97

**Eating candy doesn't cause cavities—
not brushing your teeth does.**

We are often quick to judge. We tend to be in a hurry to point fingers. When something goes wrong, we want to know whose fault it is. We *need* to know who is to blame, and then we let them have it. Sometimes we get it right. But other times, in our hurry to push responsibility toward something, *anything* other than us, we get it wrong. A lot of harm can be caused when someone is wrongfully accused. Blame is one of the easiest things to hand out and is almost impossible to take back. The damage it causes doesn't just go away. It can stay with that person for a long, long time. At its most extreme, misdirected blame can ruin a person. Don't throw it around carelessly.

By rushing to blame some*one* or some*thing* when things go wrong, we overlook our own role in the problem. It's much easier to put the responsibility onto another person than it is to honestly ask ourselves if we could have done a better job to prevent it from happening. That might require us to admit we screwed up, which, for most of us, is very difficult to do. The thing is, throwing someone else under the bus (even if he deserves it) does very little to help the situation. It creates a hostile environment, and it reflects poorly on you. Pointing fingers doesn't solve problems, it compounds them. Instead, shoulder some of the blame yourself—even when it's not entirely your fault. Admit you could have done better, and seek answers rather than creating more uncertainty. Take it upon yourself to pick up the slack where it's needed. Don't add to the problem. Be part of the solution.

When problems occur, we tend to only see their effects and rarely notice what's actually causing them. However, finding the *true* cause of our trouble is the only effective way to prevent it from happening again. We must identify exactly what we are or aren't doing, and we must fix those behaviors before any problems are going to go away. Treating symptoms will only provide temporary relief. You might get them under control for a little while, but sooner or later they'll return. If you want to put an end to the symptoms, you've got to get to the root of the problem. You've got to identify and remove what's causing them. You've got to cure the disease.

Almost as important as finding a cause is figuring out who's going to help you fix it. Recruit help from others through motivation toward a common goal rather than through shame of a previous failure. Save the blame—there's no room for it here. Strive for positive change—for yourself, for others and for the situation you're in. Stop making excuses, and get to work finding solutions. Stay focused and keep moving forward. It starts with you.

#96

Just because real life gets in the way of you hanging with your buddies like you used to, it doesn't mean you can't make up for lost time every so often.

We've talked about the balance between your friends and your parents. It is a difficult line to walk. You want to spend time with both, and peer pressure and guilt rear their ugly heads quite often during this balancing act. There is a nice, long chunk of your adolescence where your friends are king and your mother and I will be afterthoughts. Eventually you will begin to come back to us. *Eventually*. We can wait. We know the drill. We just lived that phase of our own lives. The tricky part comes when you start to realize that things with your buddies won't stay the same forever. Just as you've grown apart from them, they too have grown away from their old life with you. College, work, kids: any and all, of them can become priorities over hanging out with the guys. It's perfectly normal, and there isn't anyone who's amounted to anything in his life who hasn't had to deal with this part of growing up.

Your grandfather used to tell me all this when I was young, and I never believed him. I always thought that when he said things like this it was something that happened to *other* people. I had a tight group of friends in high school and another group in college, and even though I could hear Grandpa's voice echoing in my head once in a while, I still didn't think it was going to happen. *I was different.* Until I wasn't. It didn't happen all at once, though it felt sudden because by the time I realized what was happening, it was too late. My first job out of college required me to work a *ton* during the fall months. The rest of the year consisted of a more regular schedule, but it was also my time to catch up on all the stuff I'd neglected throughout my busy season. Time with friends was part of the equation, but so was time with family and most important-ly—time with your mother. Soon we were engaged, then married and then you came along. My main priority had suddenly arrived out of thin air and was demanding nearly every minute of my spare time. And I loved it.

We'll talk more about friends and choosing the right ones, but the reason I will bring it up is because I am experienced in that re-gard. My friends are fantastic, if for no other reason than, despite the regret I feel for not having much time for them anymore, they very rarely ever give me a hard time about it. I think they under-stand. I hope they aren't upset. I pray they don't take it personally. One of the reasons I think I'm still in their good graces is because they know that deep down I care. It's a tough thing, growing up.

The one thing that I know I have going for me in all of this, and that I hope you adopt in your own life, is the ability to make up for lost time when given the opportunity. It happens infrequently and often without warning, but every once in a while that perfect storm of circumstances starts swirling and suddenly I find myself surrounded by the friends I've missed the most, with dawn being our only enemy. Often it gets a little crazy; but I'm a lucky guy because your mother understands. Most of the time, she's right beside me. The key here is to recognize this situation for what it is, and to enjoy the chance to make up for lost time with your friends.

#95

**No matter how crappy yesterday was,
be grateful for a beautiful today.**

Some days are better than others. No matter how positive
your outlook, you will have bad days. You might struggle to find
motivation, or nothing will seem to work out, or it will feel like
everyone's against you. Those moments are difficult. They can be
deflating. It is frustrating to think about lost opportunities or unexpected problems that cost you time and money. It's depressing to
feel caught in a relentless rain storm with no end in sight. But I'm
telling you now, not only will things eventually get better, they can
improve as soon as you're ready. Even when you can't easily see it,
above those storm clouds, is a bright sun that warms everything in
its path. But the only way the sun will reach you is if you push the

clouds aside and make room for it to shine down. When you're ready to do that, you'll see the sun return.

It's not enough to say you're focused on the present and that you've moved on from the rough days. You have to *act* that way. Attack today like it's all you've got and be grateful for it, because it *is* all you have *right now*. You can't get past days back and you can't live the future days now. You can spend your time complaining about things that have already happened, dwelling on bad breaks you've been dealt, and wondering what tomorrow might bring. Or, you can put yesterday behind you, let tomorrow take care of itself, and embrace the opportunity that today presents. Don't miss the good things trying to enter your life today because you're so consumed with yesterday's clouds. Clouds will come and go, but the sun is always there above them, waiting and ready to shine.

You might be surprised what happens when you decide today is going to be a day that the sun shines on you. Things actually *do* start to work out in your favor. The answer to a problem that brought you to your knees the day before may suddenly pop into your mind, or even better, it might just work itself out. A task you were dreading may turn out to be no big deal at all. You might be treated to unexpected, but exceptional, news. None of these things are accidents. They aren't magic, either. They are byproducts of your decision to take control of your life. They are the effects of living one moment at a time, with a true appreciation for how fleeting, but important, each moment is. They are the payoff for treating each day like the blessing that it is.

As important as it is to let go of the past, you have to absorb some of it or you'll never grow. Each experience contributes to the person we become. Cherish the memories, learn the lessons, and hold on to the love you've been shown. Take in all the good, and build on it every day. Strive to create more great moments. Don't stand still long enough to let the storms stop over you. Live each new day with the hope, with the *expectation*, that it's going to be the best one yet. And then go out and make it so. You hold the power within you to create the life you want to live. No one else can impact your day like you can. Your attitude is an internal choice, something only you control. No matter how crappy yesterday may have been, today is a beautiful day. Be grateful for it.

#94

Going grocery shopping on an empty stomach is both irresponsible and dangerous.

Going to the grocery store without eating first is a good example of the damage a lack of preparation can cause. You are likely to buy things you don't need. They will probably be unhealthy and a waste of money. You might *think* you need them, but if you had gone in prepared, you'd think with your mind instead of your belly. You'd know that those products *are not* the right ones to get you where you want to be. Life is no different. A lack of preparation will lead you to do things that are a waste of time—either they're unnecessary to accomplish your goal, or they're not the most direct route there.

Not only is shopping hungry a bad idea, so too, is shopping without a list. You wouldn't go into a grocery store without at least some idea of what you want to buy, so why would you ever live your days without at least some idea of who you want to become? You've got to have a plan. You've got to set goals. It's great to have some spontaneity in your life, but if you don't have a plan for the big picture—an idea of what you want and how you're going to get there—you'll be in trouble. A plan gives you a sense of purpose, a next step. It guides you when you face tough decisions and it motivates you when you're stuck. A plan gives you the confidence that you're doing the right thing and that you're on the right track. You've thought it out, mapped your course, and as long as you follow your plan, things will work out. It requires some effort up front, but once the plan is in place, momentum takes over and each step builds off the last.

Sometimes even the best laid plans need readjusting. With a plan, you will at least know when life starts to get off track. Without one, you could easily continue down the wrong road, and by the time you realize it, turning around is a long way back. Even when it's not blatantly obvious, you'll know you're getting off course because you'll feel it in your gut. Something will not seem right. When you start to feel that way, don't be stubborn. Fix it. It's difficult to admit you've made a mistake somewhere along the way, but it happens to everyone. The truly successful people are not immune to having plans go awry. They are successful because they recognize it early, admit it's probably not the path they want to take, and make corrections as quickly as possible.

Your plan is only a guide, but it's there because at one time you thought it was the best option. Either it still is, and you should follow it, or it's not and you need to change course. Whatever you do, don't follow a bad plan just because you don't want to admit it's no longer the best way. Accept the fact that things change.

Your motivations will change. Exterior factors will change. And your plan must change if it is going to work. There is a time and place for letting loose and throwing caution to the wind. A time for putting the plan aside and just enjoying whatever life brings you. But those moments are most beneficial when they take you places you've already decided you want to go. Determine a destination. Prepare a plan. And then enjoy the ride. Just don't do it on an empty stomach.

#93

**We all have some sort of super powers,
but we don't all use them.**

Could you imagine if Superman never flew? What if he decided to ignore his superpowers? How frustrating would it be to know that someone like him existed, but that he refused to use those talents to save people and fight bad guys? You would probably feel let down. You'd wish he would take full advantage of his ability to make the world a better place. You'd be sad thinking about the talent he was sitting on, all the potential being wasted. Well, you are no different than Superman. You have your own talents and abilities and potential. If you don't tap into it—no matter what your reason is—someone, somewhere will be let down. Maybe her life won't be what it could have been had you allowed your own super-powers to shine through.

Despite what you see in your cartoons, we don't have x-ray vision, we can't leap tall buildings in a single bound, and we're not faster than a speeding bullet. Still, we all possess some sort of special ability—something that we can do better than most others. This is true for everyone, without exception. We all have something to contribute, some talent that can leave a lasting impression on the world. It might be something that ends up changing history, or it could be something that changes one person's afternoon. The scope of the impact isn't what matters. What matters is that someone else's life is better because of something we did. What matters is that we don't ignore the gifts we've been given and that we put them to good use.

Believe it or not, many people never do put their superpowers to use. Maybe they're afraid. Maybe they're unsure of themselves. It could be that they just don't realize how gifted they are. No matter the reason, the fact that there are unused talents out there is sad. It's sad that the world will never know how great that person could have been, and it's sad that the person won't feel the joy and fulfillment that comes with realizing their potential. Just like everyone else, *you* also have superpowers. The advantage you have now is you are aware that they exist. You know what's at stake. You have the opportunity to start discovering and developing those talents now so they can flourish. You have a chance to live without regret. Do it. It's much better to have taken a risk and fallen short than to not and wish you had.

Discovering our superpowers can be as challenging as using them. What are the talents we possess, and how can we make them powerful enough to affect others? How do we become the people we are supposed to become? It starts with following your interests.

We are most aligned with our purpose in life when we feel happiest. Finding the activities that you enjoy, the things that make you happy, is a key to discovering your superpowers. Pay attention to what interests you. Often the things you're most interested in learning about are the things you'll be exceptionally good at. Some people have no problem recognizing what makes them happiest. They've always known where their superpowers lie. For others, finding their true purpose is more of a journey—one that constantly evolves and never really ends. Just remember that we all have some sort of superpowers, and whether you discover yours today or ten years from now, what's most important is that you use them.

#92

Don't be afraid to see things differently from everyone else.

We were made to think. We are designed to contemplate, to wonder, and to analyze. It's one of our greatest gifts—the ability to form thoughts and ideas, to take what is and figure out a way to make it what we want it to be. Yet, as amazing as this ability is, we often ignore it. We fall in line with what others think instead of forming ideas of our own. We let someone else determine how things are and what they will become. Now, in many cases this is perfectly okay. There's no use reinventing the wheel when it works fine as it is. But, there are plenty of other instances where the whole thing would be better off knocked down and rebuilt, situations where we would all benefit if only someone would challenge the status quo. Sometimes we need a person willing to offer ideas for a newer or better or different way. It takes someone unafraid to see things a little bit differently.

In order to see things differently, you cannot allow your beliefs to be formed without your consent. You have to learn to think for yourself. You must always be shaping and developing your own ideas, your own beliefs, and your own opinions. It's important to keep an open mind. It helps to be a bit skeptical. And it's better if you change your perspective from time to time. A thousand people can see the same performance and all take something different away from it. That's part of what makes life so interesting. Everyone is unique, and from that variety comes possibility. When those possibilities are put to work, progress is made. But it only happens if everybody is allowed and encouraged to think their own thoughts, to see things differently from what's considered "normal", and to test new ideas.

It takes a courageous person to go against common thoughts and approach a problem in a different way. Often that's the *only* way difficult problems can be solved. You can't do things the same way they've always been done and expect the results to change. They need a fresh take, from a new perspective and without prejudice. Shake the systems up a little bit. Ask the questions that haven't been asked, and consider the options that haven't been considered. There will be resistance. No great change has ever come without some resistance. In fact, you might be the only person who thinks what you think, but that's okay. Don't feel pressured to conform. Whether it turns out you are correct or not, thinking differently will open eyes to other ideas and new possibilities. It will inspire others to think differently, as well.

Looking at life from a different perspective doesn't mean you should thrive on being a contrarian. Don't cause trouble for the sake of causing trouble, but do raise questions when they need to be raised. The fear of being different should not paralyze you. You can't make a difference until you see things differently. Maybe the solution lies on the road less traveled, but it will never be found unless someone is brave enough to walk that path. So walk it, and don't worry what others say. Don't ever let someone else tell you how to think, unless it's "with your heart" and "for yourself." Don't be afraid to see things differently from everyone else.

#91

Allow yourself to get lost in a good book.

People can be broken down into two types: readers and non-readers. There are some who have a neutral attitude towards reading, but most either love to read, and do it every chance they get, or they see reading as torture and want nothing to do with it. Those who read will read anything that is available to them. They sit at the kitchen table and read the entire cereal box, they read obituaries of people they don't even know, they read to hear the words in their head and to feel something, anything.

I'm a reader, and I hope that you will be as well. There is so much to gain from reading. You learn how to write, you develop your imagination, and you gain knowledge. Reading simply makes you smarter. Sentence structure, random information, and relief from real life are the spoils of the reading (wo)man. Do whatever you can to make it a habit. And, if you find yourself struggling, put the book down and choose another one. There are too many books out there to force yourself to read one you're not enjoying. And, good news, even the non-readers can be converted if the subject is interesting enough to them. As children we are often forced to read material we have no interest in and then begin to believe all reading is boring. There's something written out there for every taste and every interest. Find the material that speaks to you and dig in. You'll never look back.

When you allow yourself to get lost in a book that feels like it was written specifically for you, your mind opens up in ways it rarely does otherwise. You become engulfed in the story and live the fantasy that the author describes. While you are living and breathing the story you aren't stressing your problems. You're becoming rejuvenated, and when it's time to get back to real life, you're in better shape. The written word is one of the greatest gifts we've been given. It puts you in a one on one conversation with some of the greatest minds in the history of the world. There's something magical about the idea that a person—a writer such as Shakespeare—can speak directly to you, while you sit in your living room reading a play more than 500 years after it was written. It's the closest, most personal connection we can make with history. Not only that, it's entertaining. Why wouldn't you want to read?

Whether it's to gain knowledge, to escape reality, or to keep your brain sharp, take the time to read what interests you. No matter what else you might have going on, there's always time to get lost in a good book. Just allow it to happen. You'll be glad you did. And once you've done it once, you'll want to again and again.

#90

Treat all people with respect... girls especially.

It doesn't matter who they are, or what they do. It doesn't matter what they look like, or where they're from. *Everyone* deserves to be treated with respect. We are all on a journey, and although each journey is different, we're all in it together. We've all had hard times. We've all faced difficult challenges, but that doesn't make us any less human. In fact, our fortitude and endurance during hardship *is* what makes us human. If anything, those are even greater reasons to respect a person. Unless you've actually gone through what that they are going through, you can't (and shouldn't) judge them. And if you *have* experienced something similar, you can probably appreciate their struggle enough to know that support and encouragement is what they need most. So show them respect. Acknowledge their efforts and treat them well.

Respect begins with accepting people for who they are. They may not always act the way you want them to act, or say the things you want them to say. They may disrespect you or others, but belittling them in return is not the answer. It's natural to want to fire back, to repay their rudeness. Please don't. Resist the urge to bring yourself down to that level. Instead, show them how people *should* be treated. Encourage them to respect everyone by default. Make them aware of the pain they can cause, and let them see the benefits of mutual respect. If they are shown respect and treated with dignity, they will almost always act the same way in return. There's no reason you can't be respectful first, and let others follow your example. It starts with accepting that, although everyone is different, we're all deserving of basic human respect.

One way to immediately make others feel respected is to include them. Welcome them into conversation and listen to what they have to say. Show them that their opinions matter and that you *care* what they think. It is possible to respectfully disagree with someone, but to be honest, there's a shortage of that way of thinking in the world today. Many are quick to insult or ignore people they don't agree with. They'd rather avoid that person than work together to get to the bottom of the issue. No progress is made that way. When you appreciate a difference of opinion and include people who possess those points of view in your life you will be exposed to new (and sometimes improved) ways of thinking. You may not always choose their ideas, but at least respect them enough to hear what they have to say. You might be pleasantly surprised.

Being respectful of all people is very important. It's simply the right thing to do. But before you can show anyone else respect, you have to respect yourself first. Behave with dignity and class. Don't belittle your talents and don't question your potential. Believe that you are worthy of being trusted, admired, and respected. When you do, others will see it. And most of the time they will treat you appropriately. Like anything else in life, you cannot control how others act. You can encourage them to do certain things, but you can't force it. All you can control is how you respond to their behavior. So respond gracefully. Set the example. Treat *all* people with respect.

#89

The beaten path is boring. Find your own way.

Humankind has spent centuries discovering the most efficient ways to do things. Systems are in place to save us time and effort. Still, there will be occasions when you get the urge to go away from these systems. Maybe you think you can find a better way. Maybe you want to see it for yourself. Maybe you're just tired of following the crowd. No matter the reason, if you start to feel like it's time to do something your own way, do it! Don't think twice, don't second guess yourself, just get started. It's okay if you aren't sure exactly how you're going to do it, or precisely where you'll end up. If you just start walking, things will begin to fall in place.

All the successes, all the accomplishments, and all the great feats in human history were achieved by men and women who thought a little bit differently than everyone else. These types of people are prone to walk to the beat of their own drummer. They are not afraid of failure. They are comfortable being uncomfortable. Some may call this characteristic a curse, but those who insist on veering slightly away from the norm and stirring things up a little bit, they are the people who find greatness. Some trip over it and others get hit in the face with it, but when they find it the world is forever changed as a result.

You may not become someone who alters human history on a grand scale, and that's okay. That shouldn't be the only reason you take the uncharted path, only a potential result. The reason you go this way is because that's what facilitates discovery. It's how you learn about the world and how you learn about yourself. The trail you blaze on your own hasn't been tampered with. There is no shape, no forced direction to follow. The direction it takes is up to you. And that's where the "catch" comes in. There's always a catch, right?

The catch, in this case, is that the road less traveled is often much more difficult than the common road. It has branches in the way and there's no guarantee the route you're blazing will lead you where you want to go, let alone become the most efficient. In other words, it's very possible that your hard work won't lead to the results you had desired. This isn't the worst thing in the world. In fact, I think it's one of the best parts of making your own way. If you don't find success, most likely you've found some other things instead. Things like determination, perseverance, confidence and discipline come to mind. These aren't just minor consolations. They are the building blocks for future trail blazing. They are the characteristics of a person who will have more successes than failures, and they all come from having the courage to step off that boring, beaten path and find your own way.

#88

Be grateful for what our military does for us, not just on holidays...every day.

As Americans, we celebrate a couple military-themed holidays. Memorial Day and Veterans Day are there to remind us of the sacrifices made by the men and women who serve in our armed forces. All four of your great-grandfathers served the United States in some capacity or another. They fought in World War II and Korea. They faced some serious danger and some miserable conditions. One was a prisoner of war. They didn't do these things because they enjoyed it. They did it for me, for you, and for all the Americans still to be born who will enjoy living in a free country.

I don't know about you, but I don't need a holiday to realize how remarkable their service was. I don't need other people to tell me it's time to appreciate those men or the hundreds of thousands of men and women who are defending our freedoms as I write this or as you read it. I don't do it every day. I'm guilty of taking things for granted just like everyone else, but when I pass someone in fatigues, or see a military special on TV, or when I see a Korean War Veterans magazine on Pop-Pop's coffee table, I am reminded how lucky we are. Thankfully, there are many people who are willing to enter the military and make the necessary sacrifices. I am not sure I would be able to do what they do. To be away from your family and in harm's way on a daily basis can't be easy. I'm fortunate I don't have to.

As a result, I sometimes find myself feeling guilty. Why am I okay with others doing what I admit I don't want to do? The simple answer is this: I'm not okay with it. Fortunately, there are enough brave men and women who choose to serve that I am able to follow my dreams in a relatively safe and secure homeland. The best way I know how to honor them and show my thanks is to live consciously; knowing that everything I am able to do is a result of the sacrifices of our loved ones, and the many thousands of service people we will never even meet. I try my best not to take those freedoms for granted. I feel the pain of the families who are always worried about the well-being of their loved one. And I try to pay that awareness forward in the way that I raise you. I think, like any other human being, our service people mostly just want to feel loved and appreciated. They want to know the sacrifices they are making are not in vain.

So, the next time you walk through an airport or a shopping mall and you see a soldier in his or her fatigues, say "thank you." Tell them you appreciate all they do for you and for all Americans. Most of all, let them know they have your support and that you are proud of them. You don't need a holiday for that.

#87

You come from generations of
hard-working people. Don't let them down.

We've got it easy compared to what the generations before us had to endure. We owe a debt of gratitude to them—those who worked to exhaustion, under terrible conditions and for horrible wages. Their efforts laid the foundation for the opportunities we enjoy today. Many of them immigrated to this country hoping for a better life, and although some things may have improved, they earned everything they got. On some occasions (probably many) they went without food. And they did it all in the name of "The American Dream." It's probably true that this lifestyle offered more promise than the situation they'd left, but the sad reality is they really had no chance to truly capitalize on the dreamy lifestyle they came here to pursue. It took decades of their hard work at low-paying jobs to allow you and me a fighting shot at putting the dream into action.

That's why there's no room for coasting in our life. We have this fantastic opportunity to pursue our own greatness and it's because they did the hard work of laying the family foundation in this country. Compared to what they went through, our role is easy. Heck, our role is *fun*. It will take some effort on your part, sure. But you owe it to them to be the best person you can be. Notice I'm not saying who you have to be nor what you should do. No matter what you choose, make sure you give it everything you have. Those who put in the critical groundwork wouldn't tell you this, that generation was too polite, so I'm telling you for them. Their burden was figuring out how to make their way in this brand-new and opportunistic— if not huge and terrifying—world. And they more than did their part.

In an age of entitlement, it's important you understand that the privileges so many of us are accustomed to don't just appear out of thin air. Someone had to pay the price for them. Whether it was in dollars or sweat, everything we have been given came at someone else's expense. The generations that came before us deserve to be recognized for their selfless determination. They never did it for the recognition, they did it for the opportunity that it would give them and the generations to follow. They deserve our gratitude. They deserve our respect. But perhaps most of all, they deserve our best effort to finish the job they started. We have a responsibility to them.

Our responsibility is to make sure we do our very best to stand on their shoulders and turn that struggle into something in which we all can be proud. Whether here or in another life, they're watching you, I'm sure. And they're rooting for you. They'll help you however they can. Keep all this in mind when the going gets tough, because there's one thing you can't do—not under any circumstances, whatsoever, and that is: Never, ever live up to anything less than your potential. Try hard, make some mistakes—fail a few times, even. But whatever you do, don't let them down.

#86

Some rules are just begging to be broken.

The idea of "doing the right thing" is something I believe in very strongly. Rules, morals, and ethics exist to maintain order and provide fairness—to give everyone the same opportunity to succeed. However, I also think there are times when the intention of a rule should be questioned. This is not a free pass to go around breaking rules and getting into trouble, but I am giving you permission to question the purpose of those rules. If something doesn't sit right with you, dig deep enough to get to the bottom of why it exists, who stands to gain from it and how. If you feel like it doesn't have the best interest of the majority in mind or if it contradicts what's right, then maybe it's time for a change. Maybe the old way of thinking has run its course. Maybe it's time to start taking a closer look at the rules we're being asked to play by.

Sometimes rules are nothing more than barriers in disguise. They may appear to exist for legitimate reasons, and with good intentions, but in reality they are there to keep someone out. Or, they might be designed to limit opportunities or slant the "game" in favor of those who created them. *These* are the kinds of "rules" that are begging to be broken. As soon as the rules are no longer serving their purpose (of order and fairness), they need to be examined. Don't go around carelessly breaking them, but *do* question them. Investigate their origins and intent. Identify the parts you'd like to see changed, and put a plan into action. Ask the critical questions of the appropriate people. Do it peacefully and without promoting anarchy. Whenever possible, break down the barriers without breaking the rules.

Whether you plan to abide by, question or break down the rules, one thing you should never do is ignore them. Rules provide limits and boundaries—so you know what is acceptable and what isn't. Sometimes they are created with ulterior agendas and sometimes they're poorly designed, but most of the time they are fair and effective. When they work, rules are there to serve as a guide, providing a gauge to measure how well you're playing the game. If you are finding success and staying within the rules, you can feel confident you're doing something right. In many ways, rules will nudge you toward the most effective strategies or the least dangerous tactics. They typically aren't formed out of thin air and usually have just cause. If the rules are fair, then know them inside and out and use them to your advantage.

I'm not giving permission to break the rules, despite how poorly conceived they might be. It goes against the values I try to live by, and those I want to instill in you. Once you break one rule, it becomes too easy to do it again. That's not the reputation you want to have, and it's not the kind of person you want to be. But I *do* think it's okay to oppose unfair rules. It's admirable to seek changes when rules are unreasonable. I hope you'll stand up against those that are immoral, unethical, or that take advantage of someone else. Just remember that rules are created to maintain order and fairness, and you should respect them, no matter how badly they're begging to be broken.

#85

Learning things the hard way sucks...but you probably won't make that mistake again.

Despite what you're told, and in defiance of better judgment, there will be times you insist on learning lessons the hard way. It won't matter who is trying to help or how smart they may be or how much they may love you, you will not be satisfied unless you see for yourself. You won't believe me or anyone else until you feel the effects firsthand. You're not the only one to act this way. Some caveman had to be the first to touch a fire. Just about everything we've ever learned has come through trial and error. This isn't all bad. As painful as it may be, often the best way to truly understand something is by failing at it first. The problem comes when we

---

don't learn from our mistakes. There's no excuse for that caveman to be burned a second time.

You should never *want* to make mistakes, but because they are a major part of how we learn, they will happen. Think of them as mini-experiments. You try something and it either works or it doesn't. Then, you take what you've learned and try a new test. Gradually, you will get closer to the answer you're looking for. As a result, there is *always* something to be gained from a mistake. All mistakes have some value. You may even find people willing to help you, those who know what it's like to learn the hard way. But, if you make those same mistakes two, three or four times, the lesson you'll learn is that people aren't as sympathetic to repeat offenders. They don't feel compelled to help someone that won't help himself. And who can blame them?

Another benefit of making mistakes, aside from learning from them, is the motivation they provide. As long as you choose to view them as part of the learning process, and don't let them poison your outlook, mistakes will allow you to feel the *sting* of failure. I'm not talking about physical pain, though that plays a role as well. What I mean is the bruise your ego takes when you come up short. Hard lessons can destroy confidence if you let them, but if you use them as incentive to *not* feel that way again, you will gain something you never could have without failing. You will learn how you *don't* like to feel. You'll also realize that, in many cases, the worst really isn't all that bad. You will see there's nothing to fear.

As badly as I want to guide you and teach you lessons about life, I know there are some you'll just have to learn on your own. To stand in your way and try to protect you from those growing pains would be wrong. My job isn't to always keep you from falling; sometimes it's to just be there with a Band-Aid when you do. On those occasions, my greatest impact won't come from a wagging finger or a scowling face. It will come from a quick dust-off and words of encouragement. There is no substitute for experience. I can give you mountains of advice, but sometimes the only way to really learn is to live—even if that means finding some things out the hard way.

#84

If you never try the big shoes on, you'll never know how well you can fill them.

I encourage you to hold yourself to high standards. The higher the better, too, because underestimating your own ability is one of the greatest mistakes you can make. You will meet enough people in your life that will do it for you; the last thing you need to be is a contributor to that sadness. I'm not sure if those people are unhappy with their own lives, or regret not taking a shot themselves, but if you allow someone else to control your self-worth, you've taken the most powerful thing you have and given it away. And once you give it away, those people aren't as likely to give it back. Misery loves company and you don't want anything to do with that crowd.

There is no better time to fulfill those high standards, and become the person you envision yourself being, than when the opportunity arises to try on the big shoes. The big shoes are left over when someone who's become a success moves on, for whatever reason, and you are next in line to build on their achievement. Or maybe it's an opportunity to build your own pair of big shoes when you decide to create something yourself. It could be anything—on the largest or smallest of scales—but when the chance to step into those shoes arises, you'll know it. You'll know because you'll feel nervous. You'll feel a bit unworthy, even. You'll question yourself, and whether you're capable of being next in line. You'll worry about being compared to your predecessor; you'll worry that you won't measure up. You'll worry that you might fail. And the most honest thing I can tell you about all of this is you might be right. You might not be the best person to take over, you might not be worthy, you might be awful compared to the guy before you. You might fail. Even worse, you might fall flat on your face while you do so. But so what?

If that happens, you pick up and move on. You find some other shoes to try on. Because sooner or later, if you keep fearlessly stepping into those shoes, eventually you're going to nail it. Eventually you're going to fill them so well that *you'll* need a bigger size. Eventually *your* shoes will be the big ones someone else aspires to fill. But it all starts with that first attempt. If you pass on that chance two things will happen: 1) You won't fail, but 2) You won't be great, either. Instead, you'll spend your time wondering how you might have done, how well that risk might have panned out. You'll be so focused on that missed opportunity that you may miss another as it comes along. And once that happens, forget about it. The opportunities will dry up. They don't waste their time on people who don't acknowledge them. They find someone that will give it a shot.

I know you're capable of getting it right, even if you have to wear down the soles of a dozen shoes. Keep putting them on and lacing them up. You are equipped to fill a pair so perfectly you'll wish you'd tried them on sooner. And that's the truth. You can find the big shoes you were meant to fill—and you will. But first, you have to start trying some on.

#83

Fighting often causes more problems than it solves...avoid it if you can.

It won't take long before you find yourself in a situation where a fight seems inevitable. It might be an argument or even a full-scale fistfight. Do what you can do keep things from escalating to that point. Neither of those scenarios are constructive or ideal. In fact, they are more likely to be *de*structive and downright dangerous. The best thing to do is try to get the problem resolved in a civil manner. I know how these things work. Sometimes you're dealing with a jerk who refuses to talk about things and instead wants to yell about them. If all he's doing is yelling, chances are you're not going to make any ground, and he's either going to continue yelling until one of you walks away or he's going to get bored of yelling and decide he'd rather knock your lights out. Either way, the outcome won't be a productive one.

On the other hand, there might be a time when *you* are the jerk. Maybe you are overreacting, or letting your emotions get the best of you. When that happens it's hard to regain your composure, but it's a good idea to learn to recognize those emotions and how to get ahold of them. It will save you a lot of headaches, both figuratively and literally, if you prevent a situation from getting out of control. It wasn't long ago that a fight was just a fight. You took a beating or you gave a beating—or maybe both—but when it was done, it was done. And there were only fists involved. Now, what was once an old-fashioned fistfight quickly turns into a stabbing or shooting. People who are bested come back for more, only they do it with a dozen of their weapon-carrying friends. You don't want any part of that kind of trouble. And that's why it's so important that you recognize a situation that can be peacefully resolved from one that can't. The faster you remove yourself from those that can't, the better off you'll be.

In most cases, things are not *worse* when a problem goes unsolved. Right? You came in having the problem. You didn't solve it. Things are the same as they were before. Now, throw the consequences of a fight into the mix. Did it solve your problem? Maybe. Maybe your opponent will no longer do the things that upset you in the first place. But maybe that's because their jaw is wired shut and they're going to be in the hospital for three weeks. That's the problem with letting a fight try to solve your issues. You end up with more problems. Different problems. And no guarantee that the original problem is even solved. I'm willing to bet hospitals, lawyers, and pipe-and-chain-wielding gangs are worse problems than the original.

When you try to avoid a fight, however you go about doing it, you're going to find that your combatant won't like it. Most likely he'll call you names and try to embarrass you into fighting him. In this situation, the only question you need to ask yourself is "will knocking this guy out solve our problem *directly?*" If the answer is no (it almost always is), then you need to walk away.

#82

**If you've tried and still can't avoid a fight...
give 'em hell.**

No matter how hard you try, sometimes you just can't avoid a fight. If you've done everything you can to resolve the problem peacefully, and you're still being backed further and further into a corner, then there's only one thing left to do: You have to fight your way out. It's not ideal, but if you have no other choice, then fight. And don't just fight hard enough to get out. Fight hard enough to make your opponent understand that pinning your back against the wall was a bad idea. Force them to pay for giving you no other choice. Show them that you were the wrong person to mess with, and make sure they will never try it again. Be clear that you will not allow yourself to be pushed around, or you will always be fighting these battles.

When you stand up to a bully, you send them a message. They realize that you are not the easy target they thought you were. Chances are they will back off—because if there's one thing bullies don't like, it's a fight. But they're not the only ones who will take notice. Anyone else who witnesses or hears about what you did will also be aware that you are not to be taken advantage of. If they ever thought about testing you they will now reconsider. It's possible that fighting your way out of one corner will prevent you from ever having to do it again. Fighting will never be ideal, but something good *can* come from standing up for yourself.

Defending yourself is one thing, but when you have a family of your own, you'll feel a need to protect them as well. Something changes when you have others who depend on you. You'll see that you are not as concerned about your own well-being and will quickly put yourself in harm's way if it means taking care of your loved ones. This doesn't change the fact that all fights should be avoided when possible, but it does make it much more important that you stand up and fight when given no other choice. Doing nothing will no longer affect only you, it could also hurt those you love most. The stakes become much higher. You can't stand by and take it when others are counting on you to protect them.

I hope you never have to fight. I hope that you find a way to always settle differences in a civilized way, with a peaceful conclusion that satisfies everyone involved. But I also know that those are unlikely wishes. I realize that sooner or later you will find yourself in a situation where you have no choice but to fight your way out. There will be a moment when you choose either to defend yourself or risk being walked all over again and again. When that happens, stand up and fight. Fight for yourself. Fight for your family. Fight for what you believe. A fight is never the *right* answer, but in some situations it's the *only* answer. If a fight is the choice you are forced to make, then give 'em hell.

#81

There is something greater than us out there. Take comfort in that.

As you get older you may decide that your beliefs don't necessarily line up with the religious thought your mother and I have raised you to follow. If that happens I won't be upset with you. Changing your beliefs on religion would mean you've given them a lot of thought and come to some conclusions on your own. In my opinion, the most important religion is the one that teaches you to treat people with kindness and respect. The one that encourages you to help those who are in need and value people over possessions. The last time I checked, that was just about every religion. So what I'm saying is, go ahead and make your own rational decisions.

Follow the religion that explains life in a way that makes the most sense to you.

What's most important to me is that you believe in *something*. The beauty that exists in this world didn't just appear—it was designed by something greater than us. Understand that your life has a purpose, and that you are here to discover and fulfill that purpose. And the whole time, take comfort in the idea that the greater Being just wants you to be happy. They want you to realize your dreams and achieve success. They are not working against you; they are working for you.

One of the hardest things to understand is why things happen the way they do. There might be a time when you want something very badly, so badly that it becomes all that you can think about. And it may seem like it's especially difficult to achieve. You'll find yourself getting frustrated, and you'll remember what I'm telling you here. You'll think *"If this Supreme Being wants me to be happy, why are they making this so difficult?"* My answer is: If things don't go how you want, be patient. It's not that they're making things difficult. Sometimes they use the challenge as a way of weaning out the people that don't want things badly enough. Other times, you're closer than you realize and they're just waiting for that final push, one last whole-hearted effort from you. When you give up, whether out of a lack of faith or an abundance of frustration, you miss out on the happiness that is in store for you.

On the other hand, when the thing that you want so badly is eluding you, it may be that there is something even better in store, and had you gotten what you wanted right away, you'd stop looking or stop trying. By being elusive, the object of your desire is leading you toward a result so far beyond your wildest dreams that you don't even see it coming. This is why it's so important to keep a level head when life gets difficult. Sometimes delays are not failures, sometimes they're setting you up for the largest successes. I have seen this happen. It is real. And so is the existence of something greater than us. Take comfort in knowing that you are being looked after.

#80

There's always a way to get what you want.
Be resourceful.

The best things in life don't come easy. They are rarely ever handed to you. If you want something badly, you will need to work for it. You will need to do everything you possibly can to make it happen, and then you'll need to ask for help to finish what you couldn't do alone. And, just when you think you've got it under control, someone will tell you "no." *No, I can't help you. No, I won't help you.* You'll hear "no" more times than you care to remember in your life. You'll hear it from me. You'll hear it from your mother. You'll hear it from the pretty girl you want to take on a date. But that's okay. Keep asking. Don't be discouraged by one rejection. Or ten. Or even one hundred.

When you hit a roadblock, the most important thing to remember is there is always a way to get past it. One time you may have to go around it; another time through it may be your only option, but no matter how unlikely it may appear, there is always a way. It's up to you to find that way. It's rarely easy, but if you want it badly enough you will make it happen. What often separates people who always seem to get what they want from those who don't is resourcefulness. They know how to find alternatives when ideas are scarce.

One of the things about kids—perhaps their greatest asset—is their knack for asking incessantly and shamelessly until they hear the answer they want. While this drives most parents crazy (yours included), every time we give in so the whining will stop, it serves as proof that persistence pays off. The whining, begging, and pleading doesn't go over as well for adults as it does for children, so you'll have to rework the technique a little bit, but the idea stays the same: Pursue what you want until you have it.

There are times when even the strongest determination won't get you what you're after. That's when it's a good idea to take a step back and think about what might be the problem. It's also the time to pull out your resourcefulness. Be creative. Think differently. Try something that seems completely crazy. Often the worst that will happen is you end up where you started. Or, you could get what you were after and then some. There's always a way to get what you want out of life, but to do so you have to stick with it. You have to persist. You have to test the waters and adjust your sails accordingly. And sometimes, you have to skip the corny metaphors and just go get it.

#79

The world is a big and scary place; you can always come home.

Life can be overwhelming. It's okay to admit that. It's not a weakness—especially when you're being honest. The sad truth is it gets more overwhelming the older you get. Responsibilities accumulate, and right around the time you start heading out on your own, you realize just how difficult life is. It's harder for some than others, but trust me, no one has it easy. Not all the time, at least. Knowing that you're not alone may make you feel a little better, but it doesn't make your struggles go away. I want you to know that I understand. I know how big and scary the world can be. I've had my share of fear and concern and frustration. So I do know what it's like. And that's why it's important you know you can always come back home.

Now, before you start renting moving trucks, let me clarify. While I would never say you couldn't *really* come back home—especially if you *really* needed to—in this case, I mean it more in the figurative, "rejuvenate-your-spirit, get-your-head-together" kind of way. I'm okay with you treating home like a refuge, a place where you're comfortable and can refresh your mind, body and spirit. But it should only be temporary. Once you start leaning on it as a crutch you'll find it harder and harder to fulfill your responsibilities. Before we know it you'll be mooching off your mother and me. You'll want your old room back, and we'll have to get extra food. You'll be a third wheel in our golden years and we can't have that.

I think that most times just knowing you have a safe place you can always return to will help ease your anxiety. I hope you'll feel the support that you have, even if you aren't physically in our house. The idea of coming home, where you've hopefully always felt safe, will probably give you a boost of strength. That's because home is as much a state of mind as it is a place. It's where you understand the world, and where the world understands you. It's where you know what's expected of you and how to deliver. It's where you have nothing to fear. It's where you can be you.

The world seems to get a lot smaller and a lot more manageable once you start attacking it with confidence. It doesn't *actually* get smaller. It just *feels* that way. It *feels* smaller and it *feels* slower. And you begin to feel a part of it. You don't *need* home if you know how to create those conditions wherever you are. Convert the big and scary world to suit you. If you are uneasy, create the comfort you need. Things don't have to be perfect. They won't be. But when you need "home", even if it's not nearby, you can put your mind in that place of comfort. And most of the time that's enough.

#78

Come back anytime; but while you're out there, show the world the best of you.

I've joked that the best and worst part of being a parent is knowing that one day the kids will leave. That's a little bit of sarcasm wrapped in a whole lot of truth. When you're on the front lines of raising kids—in the midst of the long days, temper tantrums and sleepless nights—that day seems like it will never come, but like anything else in life, that faraway point in time, the one that is so distant you can barely see it, it has a tendency to suddenly show up right in your face. It's just how life goes.

So, one day you'll pack up and move out. It will be a sad day—and a proud one—for me. Hopefully, by then, you'll be more than ready for what life will throw at you. No matter how prepared you are, there will be times when things get tough. You'll be tested. You'll have to make hard decisions. And that's when I want you to think of this lesson. You'll always be welcome back at home. That's an offer with no conditions and no expiration date. But as much as coming home might help you regroup, it won't eliminate the challenges you face, and it certainly won't directly help you accomplish anything.

What coming home will do, is give you a reprieve from the hardship and a chance to catch your breath. It will give you an opportunity to prepare to attack what's ailing you with everything you have. But the escape is only temporary. Eventually, you'll have to go back. Sooner or later you'll have to face those challenges again, and you'll need the confidence to know you can overcome them. Not only can you overcome them, you can dismantle them. You can use them as a springboard to greatness. It won't be long before something of their caliber is little more than a routine test—one where you already have the answers at your disposal.

Because you'll eventually be armed with the confidence to get through any difficult situation life may throw at you, why not start off with that mindset? When you are out there, why not show the world the absolute best of you? Why not attack every day—every *moment*—with a commitment to excellence and the confidence you'll achieve it? Soon, you won't need to take me up on my offer to come back home. You'll strive for excellence, and you'll get it. Your expectations will become reality. Your life will become the one you want. You will be the person I know you can be. If the day you move out is a bittersweet one, the day you no longer need to come home is even more so. It doesn't mean you *won't* come home, it just means you won't *need* the safety net that home provides. You'll be equipped with the mental toughness to find success on a regular basis. Life will come easier more often. While this may mean you won't need me as much, I won't mind. I'll be okay, because I'll know that it means you've grown. I'll know that it means you're doing just fine.

#77

There is a day to be thankful for what you have.
It's called Everyday.

As Americans, our forefathers left us with a designated day for giving thanks. Many have worked hard to preserve the purpose of this holiday—because it has evolved to be as much about turkey and mashed potatoes as it is anything else—and they encourage time spent sharing what you're grateful for with others. It might be at a large public ceremony, or a group meeting, or maybe it's at your dinner table with your closest family and friends, but because the purposes of holidays often get lost in the celebration they've become, I think it's great that we remember *why* we are celebrating. My complaint isn't that we give thanks; it's that we wait for Thanksgiving to do so.

It's easy to look at someone who has more than you, whether it is health, wealth or love, and be resentful. But, looking at the big picture, you've got it pretty good. Yes, there will always be someone who is better off than you, but there will also be someone that has it worse. Once you understand this, and embrace the fact that you will experience disappointment at some point in your life, you're left with two choices for how to live.

The first is that you can go about your life with the idea that there is a black cloud hovering over you and that it is following you and only you around—all day, every day. Not only is this no way to live, there is no quicker way to actually create this type of scenario in your life than to believe it to be true. Psychologists call it a self-fulfilling prophecy. I call it a cop-out. Look, bad stuff happens. It happens to everyone. Sometimes, there's no explanation why. But when you dwell on those events and feel sorry for yourself, you do nothing to improve your situation. The longer you go without trying to better your circumstances, the longer you'll stay where you are. The second choice is to look at life as if every day is a blessing, and see your challenges as opportunities. Self-fulfilling prophecies work both ways. Why not use them to your advantage? Your attitude and your outlook make all the difference between the two choices.

One of the fastest ways to get things working in your favor and kick off a chain reaction, is to express gratitude on a regular basis. Thank God for the blessings He's given you. Thank friends for the nice things they do for you. Thank the stranger who held open the door even though she had to wait a few extra seconds for you to get to it. Thank your family for showing you unconditional love. Appreciate the small things we normally overlook. Be thankful for the big things we normally take for granted. Remember that it can all be taken away in a split second, and without a moment's notice. Acknowledge that you have an awful lot to be thankful for, and take the time every day to express your gratitude.

#76

Never stifle creativity—your own or another's.
Encourage it; nurture it.

From the time we are born, the creative gene is alive and well in us. On some level, and in some capacity, we all yearn for the opportunity to use it in a way that satisfies our urge to build something lasting. Creativity is the spark that propels mankind forward, allowing us to evolve and live more comfortable lives. Without it, we are cavemen. But with it—with it we are moonwalkers. We are sea divers. We are technological cowboys. We've discovered new frontiers, and then we've used creative thinking to smash through them.

The question becomes, if creativity is so important, then why is it so easily overlooked? Why are more and more schools devaluing creative thinking? When school budgets are short, why are the arts among the first to get cut? My guess is: Probably for the same reason that young children are told to think more realistically—because too few people dream. Not enough people allow their imagination to run wild, to believe in things that they've long been told were "impossible" and "childish." When people you trust as authority figures tell you to be practical, and to let go of an idea that is too far-fetched, it's easy to go along with them. But they're wrong to tell you that. And, if you listen to them, then you're wrong too.

Be aware of the loss that can occur when creativity is stifled. It's not usually eliminated in one quick strike. Instead, it's gradually discouraged, shot down or ridiculed. It's made to seem silly or unimportant, over and over until the creative instinct is repressed. Usually it happens so subtly and slowly that no one is even aware of the change. Not only is it demoralizing for the person being subdued, but it puts out a flame that may have brought the world the next great invention or cure for disease.

Thankfully, there are ways to fight back. Never allow someone to discourage your creative pursuits. There are enough people out there who understand the value that creativity offers the world. They will help to bring it out of you. And, just like you may benefit from someone providing the opportunity to let your creativity shine, there are others that need your help. Encourage *them*. Tell them that there is no idea too impossible or too crazy. And reassure them that there is nothing wrong with being a little bit different. Different thinking—creativity—is the catalyst for change. And change is what makes the world go 'round.

#75

Your laugh warms my heart, and it refreshes your soul. Do it again. And again.

As a parent, nothing makes me happier than to know you're happy. It might not mean much until you have kids of your own, but hearing your laugh is about the greatest sound there is. Life is meant to be enjoyed—despite the way it may sometimes seem—and when you laugh it lets me know you're enjoying life. At least you're enjoying that moment. And that's all life is anyway, a series of moments. Sharing a laugh with someone you love is one of the moments we should try to experience every day. How you feel will determine the quality of your day, and it's difficult to feel anything but good when you bring laughter into your life.

A laugh also has the potential to change someone else's day, and in a way that nothing else can. It's a universally understood behavior that crosses all language and cultural barriers. It's a way to communicate when there is no other way to communicate. Through it, you can show someone they have your support. You can transfer confidence and morale through a laugh. You can completely reverse the course of a person's life, and you can build long-lasting relationships by bonding through laughter. It's no mystery that your best friends will become the people you share the most laughs with. Laughter is a powerful thing.

Of course, laughter also has the potential to do great harm if it comes at the wrong time or in the wrong place, or if it is done *at* people instead of *with* them. You'll know when you're getting into this territory because your gut will tell you so. You might be laughing, but you won't feel great about it. Laughing at someone else's expense is not the same thing as genuine laughter, nor does it provide you with the same relief. It's cruel and an abuse of a terrific gift. Rather than building you up and inspiring you, laughing at someone else will leave you feeling empty and defeated. It may not happen right away, but sooner or later you'll remember the time you misused the power of laughter and you'll regret it.

One of the best things about laughing is there is always an opportunity to choose it. You could be having a bad day, but if you look hard enough—if you allow yourself to see it—there's always an opportunity to laugh. It could be the ridiculousness of the circumstances you find yourself in, or a silly scenario you come across, or maybe it's an old memory that comes back to you at just the right time; no matter where you are or what you're doing, a good laugh will improve your mood. It will remind you that your situation isn't so bad after all. It will rejuvenate your spirit and it will refresh your soul. It will propel you past the parts that aren't worth laughing at, and help you find more moments that are.

#74

Choose your friends carefully. They will impact your life, positively or negatively.

When I was growing up, Grandpa used to warn me of "guilt by association" all the time. "Be careful who you hang with," he said, "because people will judge you based on the reputation of the group you're part of. If one of your buddies is a known trouble-maker, it will be too easy for others to assume you're trouble as well." I always thought this wasn't fair—and I still do—but what I've come to realize is, it doesn't matter if it's fair or not; it's true, and therefore it's something you need to think about. When you're young, friendship is kind of something that just happens without you realizing it. You're in school with the same kids every day, and eventually you start to lean toward the children you have most in common with. At that age, sharing a couple common interests is enough to form a friendship. As you get older, the selection of potential friends grows larger. You're involved in more activities outside of school; you're aware of who's trouble and who's trustworthy. You're able to choose whom to let into your circle of friends.

The group you decide to hang with will shape your future. Those friends will influence the person you will ultimately become, and depending on whom you choose, you will either reap the rewards or suffer the consequences. If you choose wisely, you will learn the true value of loyalty, the comfort of confidantes, and the extension of love outside your family. And, if you're lucky, many of those early friends will continue to provide those qualities to you, long after you're grown. Of course, friendship is all about reciprocity, so you will be all those things to them as well. That's the magic of friendship. The essence of true friendship completely lacks the "what's in it for me" drama. A friendship built on a selfless foundation will survive. It will survive cross-country moves, new jobs, marriages, kids, arguments, personal growth, and tragedy. It survives time. In its own way, it will even survive death.

Your friends have the ability to pick you up, to encourage you, and build your confidence. They can be the most influential people in your life. Most of the time, they are. Which means you are also one of the biggest influences in your friends' lives. It's a big responsibility, being someone's friend. They count on you to do the right thing. They depend on you to do your best. They need you to be honest and loyal. Most of all they need to know you're there.

Find friends who will challenge you to be great and who will be happy for you when you become that person. Spend time with people who want the most out of life and help them get there. Create memories and share experiences that will bridge the inevitable separation that life—more specifically, that growing up—tends to cause. There's a lot riding on the selection of your friends. The good news is you have a choice. And hopefully now it's an informed choice. Let it be one that will ultimately make you a better person. Choose people that will make a positive impact on your life.

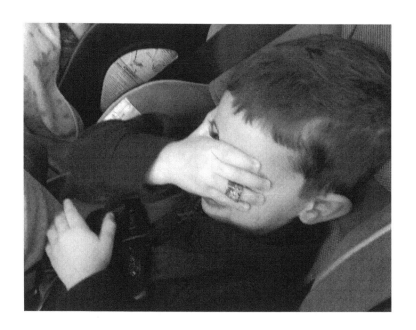

#73

Don't ever be ashamed of who you are.

You are one of a kind. An original. Someone that the world
has never seen before and will never see again after you're gone.
That is something to be celebrated. Your interests, your style, the
way you see the world—it's all so unique and special. You'll find
that people will have expectations for the person they want you to
be. They'll try to stuff you into that role and leave little room for
anything different. Please don't let them do that to you. Let your
natural personality shine through. Don't conform to what's cool or
easy or take the path of least resistance. Eventually you'll start to
realize that the easy way—the *real* path of least resistance—is to be
the person that comes naturally. It's much harder to be someone
you're not. And it's certainly not the way to happiness.

Part of growing up is discovering the person that you are. Learning about the way you think, and deciding on what's important to you is crucial in actually becoming that person. Your experiences and your environment can shape those discoveries, and they are a big part of the process, but most of it is internal. Most of it is what's naturally inside of you. It's the part that makes you unique. It's what makes you find value in life and allows you to bring joy to others. And unfortunately, it's the part of ourselves that we tend to suppress. Too often we allow other people to tell us how to be and what to like. We lose ourselves trying to become the person everyone else wants us to be.

If it's so important that we be ourselves and not try to fit a mold someone else made for us, and if being the real "us" comes so naturally if we let it, then why do so few people actually do it? Why do so many value fitting in over standing out? There's a simple answer. Fear. I know fear has been my reason anytime I've fallen in line and allowed others to decide my path. Anytime I've suppressed my true feelings, my passion, or my originality, it all stems from the fear of what others will think. It's a fear of leaving safety and a fear of potential embarrassment. It's concern that others won't accept or like the real me. It's a sad thought that so many live their entire lives under these restraints. It's a huge loss for the world that we won't ever know the greatness that those people may have possessed. Most importantly, it's a missed opportunity for those people to live happily and to realize how great life is when you live it fully.

When it comes to letting our true selves shine through, we are all a work in progress. Some people have it down pretty well, but most of us need to work at it. We need to remember that we must be happy before we can ever make someone else happy; and that the key to our own happiness is to be honest with ourselves. Embrace the person you are. Don't let shame or embarrassment get in your way. It's one thing to be ashamed of things you do or have done. Everyone has had moments they're not proud of, but if you let those moments define the person you are, you sell yourself short. Instead, use those instances as motivation for becoming the person you want to be. You're not always going to do the right thing. You will make mistakes. You can be ashamed of things you've done or mistakes you've made, but never, ever be ashamed of who you are.

#72

Too much of anything can be bad, even hair gel.

We live in a time, and a country, full of overindulgence. We overeat, overspend, and oversleep. We consume and convince ourselves it's okay. No, we convince ourselves it's not enough and that we need *more*. Most of these "things", whether they be possessions or calories or habits are not entirely bad on their own. In fact, many of them are fine, beneficial even, in moderation. But for whatever reason, moderation tends to escape us. Some is good, but *more*, more is better. I'm not sure where this comes from, but it's dangerous. This pattern of over-consumption is destructive mentally, emotionally and physically.

What's most concerning about the danger that comes from overdoing it, is the fact that we usually don't realize the harm that's coming until it's too late. We eat too much because the food tastes good, but the realization that we ate too much doesn't come until we get a stomach ache. Or, we buy something we really *want* but hardly *need,* and then it's smooth sailing until the credit card statement comes in the mail. That'll sober you up. Speaking of sober, alcohol is a perfect example of the harm that can come from over-indulging. Drinking too much will force you into another extreme: excessive apologies for the things you did and said while you were drunk.

It takes some forethought and some self-control—call it sacrifice if you want—but moderation will only help you in the long run. Usually, if you step back from the temptation and slow things down a little bit, your common sense kicks in and you can make a rational decision. Take a deep breath after you eat dinner and you'll realize you're not hungry enough for that second helping. As good as the first one may have tasted, you'll be happy you were able to walk away from the table and not carted off in a wheelbarrow.

By no means am I telling you this as someone who has this lesson all figured out himself. I'm guilty of all the things I'm warning you of, and there's millions more like me out there. Few, if any, have this one down perfectly. It's because of my knack for giving in that I feel qualified to tell you it's not worth it. Not only will you be better off without the effects of excessive consumption, you'll see how developing self-discipline can help you in all other areas of your life. It may seem like a small thing, but it is 100% true. Self-control is among the most powerful skills you can possess because it is present in everything you do. The discipline to start something when you need to start it, and stop something when it's best that you quit, will make you more productive and it will save you from many problems well before they become an issue.

#71

I won't give up on you,
even when you do something stupid.

Let's face the fact that you have done stupid things in the past, and will most likely do something stupid again in the future. What, and how stupid, they are will vary, but the idea that you're going to fall victim to foolishness from time to time is a guarantee. I've got about thirty years of experience on you and I *still* do stupid things on a regular basis. It's part of life, but not necessarily one we should celebrate. And that's where the difference lies. I don't expect you do be someone that never makes mistakes or acts foolishly, but I *do* expect you to be someone that can recognize stupid behavior (even if it's after the fact) and admit to it being wrong. I certainly don't want to find you celebrating stupid.

The definition of what qualifies as stupid is very broad. Some acts of stupidity are silly and can be laughed at, but others are much more serious and are morally wrong, if not criminal. While I expect you to never get near the criminal ones and want you to avoid the morally wrong ones, I know that things happen and that you may find yourself in a situation where mistakes are made. Often the lines of the moral issues are walked so closely and so often that they are blurred to the point where it's very easy to end up on the wrong side. When this happens, the best advice I can give is to do the best you can to fix things. Apologize for your mistakes and attempt to repair the damage they caused.

No matter how much the degree of stupid may vary in your mistakes, one thing that won't change is my support of you. I say "you" because I may not always agree with or condone what you've done, but I will always have *your* back. Keep in mind that support might not always come the way you expect it to, but when I get mad at the things you've done or the trouble you've found, it's not *you* I hate, it's your actions. You may make me angry, sad, embarrassed, ashamed or disappointed, but there is a huge difference in feeling that way towards your *behavior* as opposed to feeling that way about *you*. When you've got a love like I have for you, nothing can change it. To be clear, I am not telling you that doing something dumb is okay as long as you apologize or try to make up for it later. That is where you'll lose my support. I don't have patience for intentional acts of stupidity, especially if they are harmful to someone else. But if your intentions are good and your heart is in the right place, but maybe your judgment is off—*that* I can accept. That is a normal step in the growing up process. I'm all about you learning and there is no better way to learn than from your mistakes.

What's great about all of this is that it's usually pretty easy to realize when you've done something stupid. Most of the time, you can feel it. And if you can't feel it right away, you can usually see it in the faces of the people you've hurt. It's not a good feeling to know that you've hurt another person—especially someone you care about. But that's why it's so important to be aware when you have, so that you can do your best to make amends quickly and not let it happen again. The true test of character in a person isn't in how infrequently they make mistakes, but in how quickly they take ownership of their actions when they do. It's in the goodness of their intentions more so than their ability to execute. I believe you have a good heart, and that you want to do right. And that's why, no matter how badly you mess up, I won't ever give up on you.

#70

What's cool isn't always right, and what's right isn't always cool.

Peer pressure is a difficult thing. It's usually thought to apply only to kids—those in grade school who are easily influenced by others their age. What you'll come to realize is peer pressure doesn't go away when you hit a certain age. It won't suddenly stop affecting you simply because you're another year older. It's persistent and tireless and won't be gone from your life until you outgrow it. That's not the same as growing too old for it.

When you outgrow peer pressure you begin to understand that what's cool isn't always right, and what's right isn't always cool. You have the power and the responsibility to know the difference and act accordingly. The good news is this means you can do it anytime. You don't have to wait until you graduate or turn a certain age. You don't need to have a job, or be a parent. There is no official ceremony that removes peer pressure from your life. You decide when it's no longer relevant. Peer pressure only affects you as long as you allow it to.

The key to outgrowing peer pressure is realizing that the definition of "cool" has changed. What once might have been measured by popularity or athleticism or good looks, you come to find is better measured by kindness or sacrifice or inclusion. It matters less what others try to convince you to do and more what you, in your heart, know you should be doing. It's pretty easy to decipher right from wrong, but it's not always easy to take appropriate action. The people who stand in the way have a misguided opinion of what it means to be cool. Cool is helping others that need your help, not kicking them for being down. Cool is using your own "cool" status to talk to the new kid who might not have any friends. Cool is letting that older person know that they may live alone, but they don't need to feel lonely.

Sometimes it's hard to fit in with the crowd and still do what's right. Which begs the question: Why worry about fitting in? You might meet some resistance at first. You might feel a little bit uncomfortable. People may give you a hard time for sticking up for the person everyone else picks on. They may taunt you for speaking out when you see injustice, and when they do, you may start to think maybe they're right. They might try to embarrass you into stopping. Don't listen to them. Don't let them slow you down. If you commit to doing the right thing, even when it may not be the "cool" thing, eventually you'll start to see something interesting. Others will want to join you. They'll be glad that you set the example for them to follow, so that they can do what's right too. Suddenly you've taken this lesson and flipped it on its head. Now, what's right *is* the cool thing to do. And it's contagious. It's a social movement, and the end of negative peer pressure. It can happen. All it takes is someone like you to decide that you're going to do what's right, whether it's cool or not.

#69

Always believe, no matter how impossible it may seem, and regardless of what others may think.

Things don't always go according to plan. In fact, they rarely do. Obstacles, changes, distractions—they're all part of life. But just because they exist doesn't mean you have to give in to them. They are there to test your faith and see how badly you really want something. They only win when you stop believing. And I'm telling you to never, *ever* stop believing. Most of the time, it's that one final push that's needed to break through, but so many people get that close and then stop. They give up without ever knowing how close they were to fulfilling that dream or accomplishing that goal. You never know when that breakthrough moment could come, so you have only one choice: believe that it will happen and don't stop moving forward until it does.

It's easy to believe when things are going well, but those times when things are just so dire, and you're so beaten down, you start to lose a little faith, *that's* the moment when you have to pick it up. When you first feel the shadows of doubt creeping in, you have to remember that you hold the keys to making things better, and remind yourself that it starts with you *knowing* it's going to work out. And it *is* going to work out. Sometimes it takes a little while for the things we believe in to come to pass, but they never will unless we are so sure that we *expect* them to happen. It's during the period of uncertainty—when most others would give up—that you need to stick with it. That's what separates doers from dreamers.

For some really sad reason, people love to ridicule those who dream. They mock them, tell them they are crazy, and use words like "impossible", "never", and "ridiculous." Forget them. Just like any inanimate obstacles that get between you and your dreams, the quicker you get them out of the way, the quicker you can get on with making things happen. You don't need to be rude to those people, but you certainly don't need to listen to them, either. Thank them for their opinion, and then forget it as quickly as you walk away. Surround yourself with people who dream even more wildly than you do. Find others who won't accept "no" for an answer and who are committed to finding a way to make dreams reality.

When you commit to never giving up and ignoring "impossible", it becomes easier and easier to maintain that belief. Uncertainty gets smaller and smaller until it rarely ever turns up. This leaves you with more time and energy to figure out *how* these things are going to happen, rather than worry about *if* they'll happen. The obstacles become tangible, fixable problems instead of widespread problems caused by fear and doubt. Once you remove those self-imposed roadblocks, all the other challenges are much more man-ageable. Faith is contagious. When you have it, it grows inside you, and others pick up on it too. But before you can convince anyone else to believe in something, you have to believe it yourself first.

#68
Feeling sad is normal, but find someone to talk to about it. I will always listen.

We all want life to be fun all the time. We want everyone to be happy and there to be nothing bringing us down. Most of the time, you can just decide to feel this way and you will. But sometimes, no matter how much we try to feel happy, and regardless of all we have to be thankful for, sadness overcomes us. You may not even know where it came from or what's causing it, but you'll find yourself in the dumps and unable to kick the feeling. It's normal. It happens to everyone at one time or another. What's important is not so much *that* is happens to you, but rather what you *do* about it. Some people choose to keep it to themselves. They internalize their feelings and hope that the sadness will just go away. Sometimes it does, but sometimes that makes it worse.

Don't leave your mental health up to chance. When you start to feel upset or sad—whether you know why or not—find someone to talk to about it. Go to your most trusted friend and tell them what's going on. Ask for their support and their guidance. Listen to their advice. Let them help you to get your emotions back to a positive place. Many times just talking to the friend will do that for you. You don't even necessarily have to talk about what's troubling you. Just a simple chat with someone who understands you and loves you will get you back on track and remind you of all that there is to be happy about in life.

These sad or anxious feelings are processed much, much better when you are explaining them to someone else. Sometimes you don't even know what you really think or how you really feel until you put them into words. And then, once you start talking it all begins to make sense. If you are ever in the situation where you don't know who to go to or where to turn for help, or even just a talk, you can always come to me. No matter what it's about, don't ever be afraid to ask for my help. I know that you won't always want to talk about certain topics with Dad, and that's okay, but when it's me or no one, *please* choose me.

There are many difficult parts of life that we can't avoid, and it's crucial that we don't deal with them alone. It's likely that you will know someone who has already gone through what you're going through, and they know how difficult it is. They also probably know how to get through it. Allow them to help you. Don't try to get through the tough times alone. When you feel like you have no one else to turn to, remember that no matter what it's about and no matter how hopeless you may feel, you can always come to me. I will always listen.

#67

**Words sting longer than punches.
Choose yours carefully.**

You have the potential to do great harm or great good simply by the words you choose. A compliment or criticism can alter the course of someone's day and maybe even their life. Many times we say something without giving much thought about the effect it may have and whom they may harm. We don't always respect the power words possess and the damage they can cause. We think because they can't physically hurt someone that they aren't as dangerous to them as a punch. It's easy to understand why we think this way, but the truth is words often sting longer than punches. They rarely are forgotten and the pain doesn't easily go away. That's why it's a good idea to choose yours carefully.

When people let their emotions get the best of them, they say and do a lot of things that they wouldn't ordinarily. When we are hurt, our first reaction is to return the favor to the person who hurt us. But that usually doesn't solve the problem. Seeing them hurt might make us feel better for a short time, but it doesn't last. And when the dust settles, whether it's someone you are close to or not, you still end up feeling regret for the things you said. Many times the harm we cause lingers longer than we are even aware. People may not show outward signs of the pain you caused them, but one insult or mean-spirited comment (however innocently you may have meant it) can stick with them long, long after you say it. You can apologize, you can wish you hadn't said it, but once it's out of your mouth, you can't take it back. They can forgive you, but chances are they won't forget. However, if you take a moment to let rational thought in first, you might find a constructive way to handle a difficult situation.

When you say something using different words or a friendlier tone, not only might you avoid saying the wrong thing, but you can often turn a conflict into a positive. Progress can be made when your intent is to communicate and not castrate. But as soon as you start taking petty shots back at the person, you do two things: 1) you add to the problem and 2) you remove any hope of getting through to them. The focus then becomes who can win a battle of insults. When this happens, no one wins.

The good news is as easily as your words can do harm, they can also do good. They can make someone's day or redirect the course of their life in a positive direction. Rather than use the power of your words for revenge, why not use them to build people up? Use those words for encouragement and inspiration. Offer compliments and help for those who are in need. Spread a message of kindness and humanity, even if the recipients don't necessarily deserve it. You may change them. You may not. But you'll definitely feel better for it.

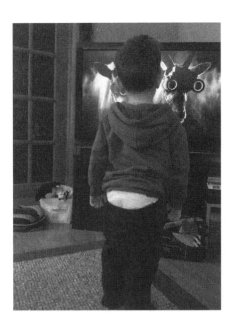

#66

God gave you a waist for a reason— it's where your pants go.

I know that there will be fads and fashions that appear to be cool to you, especially when you're young and trying to find yourself, but please think twice when it comes to which ones you choose to participate in. Some of them are harmless and fun, but others make it easy to compromise your character. They may give off an impression of you that is wrong or misleading. As a result, you're likely to be judged and labeled before you've had a chance to present the real you. The opinion that others have *does* matter and you should want them to respect you and think highly of you, your integrity, and your character.

The decisions you make about your appearance have as much impact on how you're perceived as anything else you do (often more than your actions), because how you look is typically the first thing people notice. It's almost impossible not to form an opinion of someone based on a first impression, and however inaccurate and misinformed it may be, people seldom change their initial judgments. Giving them something good to latch on to at first is huge. Put your best foot forward, every time, because you never know who is watching.

When making decisions about your behavior and appearance, it's easy to underestimate how far-reaching the effects of those decisions can be. Not only are you representing yourself, you're also representing your family. You're a walking reflection of how well (or not-so-well) your mother and I raised you. When you make a bad choice, our reputation is damaged as well as yours. When you make a good choice, we look like super-parents. As you grow up, you'll represent other entities, too. Your school, your teammates, and your employer all will have a stake in your actions. Do bad, and you let them down as well as yourself. There are plenty of people who are counting on you to do the right thing and be a person of high integrity. Work to build this reputation in everything you do.

There's a lot to think about when it comes to managing your reputation. Mistakes will happen, but if you're careful, they won't happen often. Giving a little thought to what you're doing and who may be affected by your actions will limit the mistakes. When in doubt, err on the side of caution. It's not worth sacrificing something as important as your character or your integrity for a short-sighted decision. Living in the moment is great for many things, but when you make poor judgments in those moments, you often end up paying for them long into the future.

#65

I'll love you no matter who you love.

You can't control who you fall in love with. And I don't think you should try. True love is a rare gift—one that you can't create if it's not there and that you will have a very difficult time hiding if it is. It's the strongest emotion in this world, and I believe it's one of the few things you can take with you when you leave. For these reasons, if no other, don't try to deny or ignore it. Welcome it. Search for it. And when you find it...embrace it. Don't let it go, either, because it's not guaranteed to return.

As someone who's seen how uplifting pure love can be, I will never stand in your way of experiencing it. If you are involved with someone, romantically or otherwise, and you love their company, you'll have my complete support. I don't care about their race, color, creed, gender, or any other demographic category you can think of that may be different from yours. Love does not see those differences as barriers, so who am I to become one in their name? They are superficial differences, and are transcended by just about anything else you might have in common with that person. People who grant them power are either narrow-minded or afraid. Or both.

Unfortunately, there are many people narrow-minded enough to find fault with love shared between people who are different—or not different enough. Thankfully, most keep their opinions to themselves; however, not everyone is so considerate. If there is one concern I have regarding differences between you and the person you may fall in love with, it's the challenges you may face as a result. Although you'll have my support always, there is little I can do to control how others will treat you. Whether it's a bi-racial relationship or same-sex marriage or any other mix of differences, it saddens me to know that you'll have people you've never met disapprove of your choice and chastise your behavior. It breaks my heart to think your children may be subject to that or worse. Still, love really does conquer all, and those who judge (and tend to live in extremely large glass houses of their own) should not be given the platform to stand in its way.

Because there's always an exception to the rule, I am going to reserve the right to object to you loving a certain kind of person. This person falls in none of the demographics we've talked about and all of them at the same time. The person I will not approve of you being with is someone who is of bad character. Someone who treats you poorly, who doesn't respect you, or who simply isn't a good person will *not* get my blessing. If their moral compass is off, if their priorities are out of whack, or if your well-being is a distant second to theirs, I will have a hard time being supportive of the relationship. And just the same, I expect that you'll treat them with a mutual love and respect. Other than this one condition, you have my blessing to go out and find love. Follow your heart and see where it takes you. No matter how it turns out and no matter who you fall in love with, I will still love you.

#64
Always keep a level head, especially when people around you are overreacting.

The ability to keep your composure is a skill that will serve you well, especially during tough, stressful times. When things don't go as planned or when disaster strikes, people are likely to panic. And when that happens it's nearly impossible to constructively solve the problem. You can do yourself—and others—a great favor by keeping a level head in those situations. No matter how stressed, scared or panicked you may feel, a calm demeanor is critical in getting things back under control. Great leaders shine during times like this, and it starts with being composed under pressure.

Rational thought escapes people when they overreact. Their behavior is extreme and generally unwarranted. They also tend to be all over the place. They don't know what they want or how to get there. As a result, they need someone to be their voice of reason and to show them that panic is not the answer. They need a reminder that the problem won't solve itself and that they must control their emotions. Most of all, they need someone that will tell them everything is going to be okay, and here's what they have to do to make it so. Make yourself that person. Create a reputation of being someone others can rely on for composure and stability. When you set an example of calm, others will easily follow. People are naturally drawn to someone who is assertive and steps up to take control of a situation. If you prove to them that you are that person, not only will they join you in your fight to correct a difficult situation, they will stick by you when adversity strikes again in the future. You may present yourself as the voice of reason, but if you don't have people who trust you and are willing to follow your lead, you will not be successful and the panic and disorder will continue.

Keeping a level head is not easy. It's easy to say you will, or look back and say you should have, but in the heat of the moment, it's difficult. When you're in that situation—when chaos is trying to take over—it's normal to want to let your emotions get the best of you. It might even make you feel better if you do. But that feeling doesn't last very long and the original problem will still be waiting for you. Instead, see problems as a challenge. Consider them to be a test of your character and your ability to restore order. Know that you have two options: give in or get better. Anything else is only delaying the inevitable. The challenge will remain until you correct it, and relying on others to do it for you will often lead to disappointment. Instead, be proactive and make something happen. Trust your instinct and follow it with confidence.

This attitude—a calm approach and careful thought before you react—will eventually become a habit. You'll get so used to acting rationally when faced with a problem that you won't think twice about it. Before long, the things that used to be challenging won't even show up on your radar. And that's how you grow. We don't get better by never being faced with difficulty. We get better by attacking it head on, by not letting it rattle us and by not changing who we are.

#63
Yesterday's failure leads to today's success.

You are going to experience failure in your life. In fact, I hope that you do. If you never fail, you aren't testing yourself. Failure is a sign that you're on the verge of getting better. It means that you've found your limitations and can work toward exceeding them. Not only does it help you gauge where you are, it shows how you can improve. Through failure you learn what works and what doesn't work. It is a building block to success, and one that is effective, if not necessary. Unfortunately, it's not easy to see through the disappointment of failure, and it's common to ignore its benefits; but once you finally realize what's to be gained from it, you will never look at failure the same way again. Rather than frustration, you will see opportunity.

Every failure gives us an opportunity to react in two different ways. We can accept it and quit, or we can process it and grow. I think you'll agree that it's best to try to learn from our failures and get better. Quitting is almost always the wrong decision. Still, the decision to use your failures as a learning experience is easy to say and hard to do. When you put your heart and soul into something and it doesn't work out the way you wanted, it's discouraging. It sucks the life right out of you. It becomes very easy to walk away. And even though you know that's the wrong response, and that nothing great is ever accomplished without at least some struggle, it's still tempting to give up. That's when it's most important to recognize the opportunity before you. There is no feeling like the satisfaction you get after finally achieving something that's eluded you. You're often closer than you realize. But you'll never know just how close unless you refuse to quit.

Quitting is really all that allows you to fail. That's what makes it permanent. But, if you commit to keep trying until you succeed, then failure is nothing more than a stop on the path to success. One of the key things that people often lose sight of is the process that was taken to reach that success. They see someone who has done well and accomplished much, and they think it happened overnight or without struggle. It very rarely happens that way.

Instead, it's more likely that the successful person overcame many challenges and failed numerous times before they got to the level of achievement we see them at. But you don't hear about the grind. The hardships usually aren't made public, and they certainly aren't celebrated. These struggles are faced with little attention from the outside, and encouragement is minimal. The successful person pushes through failure because of their own desire to succeed. It's usually not until they've persevered that their efforts are noticed. But when that moment comes, there's nothing like it. And it makes all the hard work worthwhile.

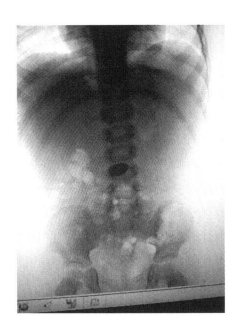

#62

"Put your money where your mouth is"
is not a literal expression.

Our culture is overflowing with sayings and expressions that are useful in different ways. Some are full of wit and sarcasm; others are ridiculous and make little sense. Buried among them are tiny pieces of wisdom based on hundreds, if not thousands, of years of history and learning. They are nuggets of truth that we can use to make our days and lives easier, or more enjoyable, or in the case of some sayings, help our lives make sense. They can be invaluable to us, especially if we know how to put them to use.

Before we can put the expressions to use, we have to do our best to understand what they mean. It's important to determine which carry deeper meaning and which are to be taken at face value. Often, the expressions that seem to be simple and straightforward can apply to many different situations and in many different ways. Whittle them down to their core and see how the message applies to you and to your life. You may find that the same expression means something different to you now than it did ten years ago or than it will fifty years down the road. Not only is that normal, it's part of what makes life so exciting. Life, and our perspective of it, is always changing.

The lessons we learn don't always carry some deeper meaning. Sometimes things just are the way they are, and there is no explanation for it. But many times, especially when age-old expressions and proverbs are involved, there is much to be learned. They are full of warnings, advice, honesty and foresight. Failing to see the wisdom in these lessons is a great loss. Conversely, using them to guide us can provide a great advantage. You may not completely realize how valuable this can be until one applies directly to your immediate situation, but when you do you'll be grateful. Such an experience may also inspire you to take advantage of all the other wisdom you normally overlook.

This can help you in another way, too. It will encourage you to avoid blindly trusting what people say. Before you accept anything as gospel, think about it carefully. See how well the thought or idea meshes with what you believe. If it doesn't align with your ideals, either you or it will have to change before anything can be gained. If it *does* fit in with your values, then make it part of your life. We live in an age where very few things are happening for the first time. At least in a broad sense, there's always an example or a precedent we can fall back on to guide us. That knowledge is accessible, forever preserved in time-tested, highly-informative expressions. Put them to good use, that's what they're there for.

#61

If you make a mess, clean it up.

In its simplest form, you've been learning this lesson since you started playing with toys. If you dump them out, pick them up. If you spill the milk, grab a towel. As obvious and basic as this may seem, there are some times when it will be the last thing you want to do. Do it anyway. You may think someone else is more responsible for the mess and they should clean it up. Clean it anyway. You might even tell yourself that it's not so bad and it can wait until tomorrow. Don't wait. If you make excuses now, you will always find an excuse. A small spill or messy toys may not seem that bad, but they contribute to the big picture by helping you to learn discipline and develop character. Those two traits are defined by how you handle the small, seemingly unimportant tasks.

Toys strewn and milk spills are the more literal messes, but a "mess" can also be a situation that has gotten out of hand or a relationship that has been damaged. They may not be as literal, but are still very serious—maybe more so than the physical messes. And they certainly can benefit from someone deciding to clean them up. Disagreements, conflicts, and accusations are all "messes" that could probably use some cleaning. While it's not your job to solve all the world's issues, it is all of our responsibility to help where we can. If you have a role in it, focus on how you can resolve it. Compromise is usually a good place to start.

This is especially true if you are directly involved in the creation or evolution of the mess, but it also applies if you witness a problem and think you may have a solution. Be careful with this advice, as sticking your nose in places it's not wanted is normally not well received. Definitely don't pry or butt into things that are none of your business, but if after observing a problem, you think you may know how to resolve it, try to find a way to help. Should you begin to feel your help is not wanted, that's your cue to step away. As difficult as it may be to understand, sometimes people just don't want to be helped.

The desire to fix problems is an admirable quality. A person who stands with integrity and self-confidence, openly working to correct a problem they've contributed to, is inspirational. Don't be afraid to do this—often you'll find people will respect you more as a result. Not only is it the right thing to do, but making the effort to fix a wrong is the first step towards progress. The situation won't improve if there are remnants of a conflict in the way. It's a simple concept, but not always an easy one. No matter how big or small the "mess" and regardless of who is responsible for it, do what *you* can to clean it up.

#60
Take responsibility for your actions.
Yes, even farts.

It may not always be the easy thing to do, but often it's the right thing to do. If you did something that hurt someone else, accept responsibility for your actions. Then, take whatever steps you can to fix the damage. It takes a brave person to admit when they've done wrong, and an even stronger person to apologize. Although it may feel like you're showing weakness when you do, being unafraid to admit to your wrongdoing is a sign of strength. It displays character and class. It exudes confidence in your ability to overcome the challenge. And it demonstrates a desire to do what's right, even if you need a second (or third) chance. These qualities are meaningful, so don't disregard them.

Sometimes an apology, or even an attempt to repair the damage you caused, may not be enough to put things back how they were. The pain may be too severe, the cut too deep. The damage may simply be irreparable. It's unfortunate, but that doesn't mean you shouldn't try. We all make mistakes and do things we're not proud of, but an honest effort to undo any trouble you cause will at least show you care. It will help those affected understand that you didn't *mean* to hurt them. And it will encourage them to trust you again in the future.

There may be times when you feel inclined to accept some of the blame even if you don't completely deserve it. Leaders will often accept responsibility for failures that occurred under their watch. This isn't always fair, but as someone who typically gets more credit than they deserve when things go well, leaders know that this comes with the territory. As decision-makers, they are responsible for the people they lead. I'm not advising you to routinely take responsibility for things that you didn't do, but sometimes it pays to shoulder the brunt of the blame despite how uncomfortable, embarrassing or frustrating it might be. It makes others more likely to follow your lead, and less likely to dodge their own responsibilities. More importantly, it can trigger a culture of problem-solving rather than finger-pointing, which will make similar problems less likely to occur again.

Whether you stand up and accept responsibility or decide against it, it's never a good idea to blame others. Finger-pointing is a waste of time. It does nothing to fix the problem. You may not want to accept responsibility for something someone else did—and you're not required to—but rather than complain about their actions (or inaction) use the opportunity to help find a resolution. It's too late to take back what's already done, but it's never too late to start fixing it.

When we talk about what makes up a person of high-character—someone that others admire and want to emulate—honesty and integrity are at the top of that list. When you have integrity, taking responsibility for your actions comes naturally. Soon you'll realize that it's not nearly as scary or as difficult as you once thought. Hopefully, it also inspires you to do wrong less, making you a better person in the process. Others will notice. And they'll respect you for it.

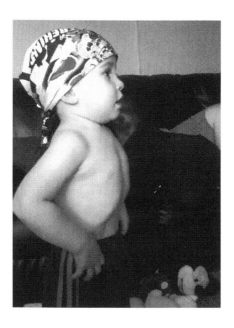

#59

Take care of your body. You only get one.

Don't underestimate how important it is to take your health seriously. Take care of your body. Watch what you eat. Exercise often. Do everything you can to maintain a healthy lifestyle, because it can be very dangerous if you don't. Health problems can affect your job, your family and your ability to pursue your goals. They can also end your life. We often don't realize we're headed toward trouble until it's too late. At that point, fixing our problems takes more work and is more invasive than just preventing them in the first place. The damage doesn't happen all in one day, or even one week, but over time it will catch up to you. And when it does, it is very hard to correct—if you have a chance to at all.

When we get busy with life and responsibilities, our health is among the easiest things to neglect. It takes time to prepare healthy meals. It takes time to go to the gym or go for a walk. And if there's anything we seem to have less and less of, it's time. Please make the time to take care of yourself, because it will only help you when you need to call on your body for endurance during a long work day or when you're fighting off a cold. A healthy body is crucial in allowing you to do all the things you enjoy, and critical in getting you through the things that you don't. When you allow your health to slip, you limit your potential and you make life more difficult.

Your body is the vehicle that moves you through life. You go as it goes. The more intact it is and the more efficiently it's running, the easier it will be for you to do what's important. Not only does a healthy body have a positive physical effect on you, it also affects you mentally. Consider the time you spend on it to be an investment in your physical *and* mental well-being. Fine-tuning your body is a key component to getting your mind right. It helps you organize your thoughts. It releases stress. When you eat right and exercise you feel good. And when you feel good you are more likely to find success.

You can't always control what happens to you, and illness, disease or accident will sometimes show up uninvited. Because this part is often out of your control, focus instead on doing well with the parts you can control—things like diet, rest and exercise. Invest in healthy behaviors. Stay away from tobacco, drugs and alcohol. Your body knows when it needs to slow itself down, so listen to the cues. Treat it with respect and it will serve you well. And *definitely* don't take it for granted. It's the only one you have.

#58

Glasses come in two kinds: rose-colored or doom-and-gloom. Which will you wear?

Every day when you wake up you have a choice to make. You can see life through rose-colored glasses, and find the good in all things, or you can choose to wear the doom-and-gloom glasses, where you expect the worst to happen. Some may tell you that it's dangerous to be an optimist. They would say that optimists will eventually lose touch with reality and live in a fantasy world, a world where nothing bad can ever happen. I say if you don't at least hope for that, then what hope do you have?

As children, we start off with a belief that there is no such thing as impossible. We see miracles all around us and we don't question them for a second. Then, as life starts to beat us down, and we see others who've given up, we begin to let doubt creep into our thoughts. We begin to think that maybe something really *is* beyond our reach or that it's not meant to be. It doesn't take long before those thoughts become our norm. Those glasses, the doom-and-gloom ones, they're worn too often and by too many. And, for whatever unfortunate reason, many people would be happy to share them with someone else. Don't let them share with you. Once you start seeing life that way, it's very hard to change.

Not only do I hope you'll always see possibility over defeat, I hope you'll help others to see it as well. As hard as it is to change once you've bought into a certain way of thinking, motivation from others is a great way to try. Hope is contagious and empowering. It makes people feel good and encourages them to take action. When someone is exposed to optimism it rubs off on them and gives them strength to believe, too. And once enough people start to believe, that's when amazing things can happen. Suppose you've been wearing the doom-and-gloomers lately and are finding it difficult to stay positive, let alone believe in the impossible. You can fix this by starting small. Notice the beauty in the world. Pay close attention to all the amazing things that are around you every moment. Appreciate what you've taken for granted. Avoid negativity by paying attention to your thoughts and feelings. Decide that this is how you want your life to be.

More than anything, optimism is a decision. It's a decision to see life with the glass half-full, and confidence that you're going to find a way to fill in the rest. Eventually this will become natural, and instead of worrying about something not working out, you'll spend your time making it happen. And if it doesn't, at least you'll know you gave an honest effort—one not persuaded by fear or doubt. When you take this route there is nothing to regret, and therefore nothing to fear. Still, it's an ongoing decision that you have to make, day after day after day. There are two kinds of glasses. Which will you wear?

#57
Write often. It's the best way
to find out what you're thinking.

This might seem strange at first. Shouldn't you just *know* what you're thinking? I see why it could be confusing, but anyone who has written—even just a little bit—will understand and most likely agree. Our brains are so over-stimulated, and must process so much at once, that it's difficult to find time to open them up and see what's really inside. Writing lets our thoughts flow freely. When you get in a rhythm, those thoughts come from deeper and deeper inside your mind. Often they are ideas you didn't even know were there. They may surprise you, but you will probably find yourself agreeing with them, because they are, indeed, yours.

What you do with these thoughts and ideas is up to you. Sometimes you might spit out random, isolated things that have little value to anyone but yourself. But other times you may realize something powerful—something that can help another person— and that's when writing to discover your thoughts can really get interesting. Many historic artists and authors have said that they were merely an instrument that collected the ideas and put them on paper. They believed something greater was working through them to create the amazing work they've left us. It's likely that they were actually doing the creating, but that it was coming from a place so deep inside of them—their subconscious—that it *felt* like it wasn't them. This is what athletes call being in "the zone."

Writing can get your mind into "the zone" in a way that even thinking can't. At first, when you sit down and just write whatever comes to mind, your thoughts will be random and scattered—a diarrhea of the brain. But eventually you'll start to see a pattern. You'll be able to look at what you wrote and know if you are feeling happy or sad, angry or anxious. You can then get down to the bottom of those thoughts and try feeling less sad, or searching for more of what makes you happy. Rather than just feeling the pain, you'll begin to understand what's causing it.

The idea that you don't know your every thought right now is scary, and wondering what those thoughts *could* be is even scarier. But if you take the time, on a regular basis, to pull your ideas out and put them on paper, you might be pleasantly surprised with what you find. You could learn something new about yourself. You may have something special to offer the rest of us. You might just end up feeling more relaxed. It could be all of these things and more. But you'll never really know unless you find a way to tap into the depths of your mind—the parts that are buried beneath emails and texts and gossip. That's the good stuff. And the best way I know to get there is to write. Just write.

#56

Playing catch with Dad is much more than throwing and catching; it is much more than a ball and a glove.

One of the most enjoyable parts of being your dad is the time we get to share together. The activities might change as your interests evolve, but being together is what's most important. This may be difficult to understand until you're a parent yourself, but having a relationship with you is my most important job. Too many fathers and sons lack a relationship with one another. They might coexist, maybe even talk once in a while, but there is no connection, no bond. There are many reasons why it might get to that point, and not all are someone's fault, but it's an awful thing no matter how it happens. And it doesn't have to be that way.

People aren't going to force us to spend time together; they're not going to make us be friends. It's up to us to make sure we continue to stay close. That's not always easy to do. We are busy. We have responsibilities that pull us away. As you get older, it will only get harder and harder. You'll be involved with more things. You'll have friends, girlfriends, and one day, a family of your own, who will all be fighting for your time. Our moments will get fewer and further between. That's how things go sometimes. So we make the most of the moments we have, and we do our best to make them happen as often as we can.

I'm willing to do what it takes for this to happen because being close with you is a big deal to me. It's important because I want to know about you. I want to know what gets you excited and what makes you sad. I am interested in the person you are and the person you'll become. I look forward to the many talks we will have as you get older and your thoughts become more independent. There are so many ideas and experiences I want to share with you, and they will come in time, but the simplest things are the ones that count the most. Just sitting next to you is enough to put my soul at ease.

So when we're out throwing the ball around, or when we watch a game, I hope one day you'll realize there's much more going on than just throwing and catching. The score is irrelevant; the moment is what counts. I know this may all seem a bit silly to you. You might be thinking *Dad's getting dramatic again.* That's okay. I would have thought the same before you came along. But if there's one thing you've taught me, it's how enjoyable life can be when there's a little one to share it with. It wakes you up to the smallest, but most meaningful, things. It redefines love. You may also be wondering if I learned all this through a game of catch. And the answer is no. I learned it watching you smile when I gave you my time.

#55
Childhood passes too fast as it is. Don't rush it.

You're only a child once, and for such a short time. Before you even realize how special that time is, you're thrown into adulthood. And once that happens, you can never really go back to being a kid. Sure, you can keep the child in you alive, and I hope that you always do, but it's never the same as life as a little boy. It's the innocence that kids have that makes childhood so special—when you have yet to be exposed to the evils of the world, and where you can get away with believing in the good in people. Eventually you'll notice that life as an adult is rarely as simple as it was when you were a kid.

That's why it's so important to enjoy your childhood. Run through the sprinkler, roll down a hill, ride your bike all summer long. Live those moments for as long as you can, because they're fleeting. You'll be a grown up before you know it, but just because it will one day happen doesn't mean you have to hurry it along. It's normal to wish you were older so you can do the things adults can do. But if you learn just one thing from me, I hope you learn to live in the moment. Wherever you are, *be there.* There will be plenty of time to drive cars and stay up late and eat what you want, so for now, focus on make believe and story time and climbing trees. This is the purest form of living, so make it last.

Even though I want you to stay a child for as long as possible, I understand that I can't keep you there forever. It will happen gradually—so much so that we'll barely notice—but one day you'll stand before me a man. Your childhood will be behind you—a series of lessons learned and fond memories that will fade over time. But no matter how much those memories fade, they'll stay a part of you forever. They'll be kept in a corner of your heart, waiting for you to call on them again. They've done their job by then, having shaped you into the man you became, and they'll guide you into the choices you make later on. This, if for no other reason, is why it's so important that you make your childhood one of adventure and discovery and learning. It serves as the foundation for the rest of your life. It sets the tone for the person you will become.

We don't want you to rush your childhood and wish it away, but at the same time, you can't hide from growing up, either. It's a careful balance to stay young at heart and also be a mature adult. Many have found the balance, so it can be done. It starts with knowing when the time has come to transition away from life as a child and start to accept responsibility. It's sad to leave those days behind, and although you don't have to completely, once you start to let them go things are never really the same. That's okay, though. Growing up is part of life, and it has its advantages too. It means you can start to stretch your legs and grow. It's a chance to see the world outside the fishbowl you grew up in. The key, as you accept that it's time to move on, is to realize that although you may be growing up, it doesn't mean you have to grow old. And should you ever find yourself growing old, and forgetting what childhood is like, go to that place in your heart where those memories are stored and let them bring you back.

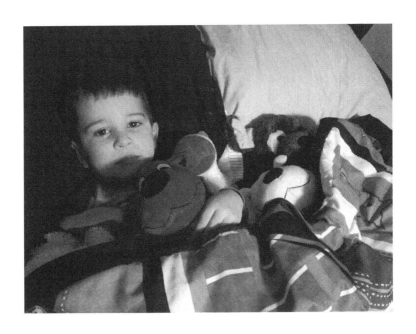

#54

I will worry about you no matter where you are and no matter what you're doing.

As your dad—and someone who loves you—it's my job to worry about your well-being and safety. No matter where you are and no matter what you're doing, I will worry about you. The world is harsh and unforgiving. It's also extremely dangerous, and it seems like it's only getting worse. There may be times when it feels like I'm being overprotective—and there probably will be times when I am—but I hope you can learn to trust my judgment and at least try to understand it. Children are getting shot in school, teenagers are driving drunk, and drugs are evolving and are deadlier than ever. It's a tough time to be a kid, and it's even harder to be a concerned parent.

I understand that it can be embarrassing to have your mom and me ask questions about where you're going and who your friends are. I know that some of those friends may not have to explain themselves as much as you. I'm sorry you have to deal with that, but I won't apologize for asking. There's a lot of bad out there, and it doesn't take more than a moment of opportunity for it to find you. Sometimes it will find you even if you don't want it to. I may have complete trust in you and your ability to do the right thing, but there are millions of other people out there and all it takes is one bad decision by them to cause you harm. I know I can't protect you from everything, but that doesn't mean I won't try.

Even when you're safely at home, I will be concerned for you. I will worry about your future. I will worry about whether your mom and I have done a good enough job preparing you for the ups and downs of life. Someone once told me that your babies never stop being your babies and you will worry about them for the rest of your life. They were right. So, even though I go about my days confident that I'm doing my best and hopeful that you'll be okay, the concern will never completely go away. You will never be able to get rid of me entirely; the best you can hope for is to learn how to tolerate it.

Despite all of this, I do understand that I can't hover over you, and eventually I'm going to have to back off. There will be a day when you are entirely your own person, and all decisions will be yours. By then I hope you've learned enough to make smart choices. You can always ask my opinion—and I will gladly give it—but ultimately it will be up to you. Still, even though you may be on your own, and the benefits or consequences of your decisions will be yours, it doesn't mean I won't be watching. And you can be sure that if I'm watching, I'll be worrying.

#53

We men are a different breed—
you can't always expect women to understand.

As men, we do weird stuff. We make strange decisions and say things that earn us funny looks. Girls don't always get it, nor should they. The things we do are *different*. They're inexplicable. And, at times, we make the girls' lives more difficult. It's no wonder our actions confuse and sometimes anger them. You will spend most of your life trying to better understand women, and just as it is difficult for you to figure them out, so too, is it hard for them to understand you. It's a mystery for sure—how two genders of the same species can have so much attraction to (and at the same time so little understanding for) the other. I wish I had an answer for you. I wish I knew why we are sometimes so opposite. I don't, but

I do know that you can get along in life pretty well just by knowing (and accepting) that there will be differences—some really big, some small and silly, but there will be differences.

Just so we're clear, I'm not blaming men or women for this disconnect. It's not always someone's fault. Some things just are the way they are. Men and women will probably always have some sort of communication barrier between them. But just because the barrier exists doesn't mean you can't try to find a way around it. Communicating with women will be a major part of your life. Your mom, your sister, your girlfriend, wife, teacher, coworker, friend, boss—they all are, or could be, women. Without at least some effort to understand and be understood you will find yourself mad, sad, frustrated, confused, disillusioned, bitter or distraught—to name a few. Often, you can minimize these emotions by your willingness to see things from their point of view. This doesn't mean you have to agree or concede, just make an effort to speak in the same language.

It's easy to allow a misunderstanding to get in between us and our loved ones. And really, a lack of understanding someone else and their opinions is not limited to gender differences. As men, you and I may also have problems communicating with one another. This isn't a new thing. Fathers and sons have been butting heads since the beginning of time. Unfortunately, it's also common for these misunderstandings to turn into big fights—fights where miscommunication is no longer the problem, because they stop communicating, period. Whether it's with me, your mom or your future wife, don't let a small misunderstanding set off a major conflict. Get down to the bottom of things before they escalate.

When it comes to relationships with those close to you, life is better (and smoother) when people understand what motivates you. You can't just expect them to understand, you have to *make* them understand by explaining why you do what you do and why you like what you like. Don't assume they'll know how you feel; assume that they don't and then communicate it to them. Show them what the view is like from your perspective. Once they see where you're coming from, they just may begin to understand you.

#**52**

If you don't use it on a regular basis, your imagination will leave you. Getting it back is hard.

When we're kids, our imagination is remarkable. There is no such thing as impossible; nothing is too farfetched. We are at the mercy of our minds and we love every minute of it. It can take us places we'd never otherwise go, or remove us from situations we couldn't otherwise get away from. It's like a toy you can bring with you anywhere. It's the driving force behind our dreams. And, if we're lucky, it's a preview of our future. With a strong imagination you can create any existence and experience it in detail. Your imagination has no limitations. That is, unless you ignore it. As you grow older some might encourage you to put your imagination to rest. People may say that imaginations are reserved for children and that the adult world doesn't have room for dreamers. In reality, not only *does* the world have room for dreamers, it *needs* them.

So much of the progress we've made is the result of adults with active, unrestrained imaginations. They see the world through the same wide eyes they did as a kid. They never let go of their natural ability to believe the unbelievable, and they never questioned their ability to make it happen. Those people have pushed their minds well beyond what's practical and have believed strongly enough to see their wild ideas come true. The problem doesn't lie with the person who dreams big, it lies with the person who tries to stop them. If we don't continue to encourage that type of thinking, especially in young people like you, it will slowly leave. And once it does, it doesn't come back easily. Not only do I hope you keep your imagination alive, I hope you will encourage that from others, too.

One of the reasons children have such strong imaginations is because they use it often and, like a muscle, the more you use it the stronger it gets. Children use it so often that there is a very fine line between their "make-believe" and their reality, one that they can expertly cross over back and forth in a moment's notice. To them, it's all the same world—one where they can do or be anything they want. To adults, they may seem to be disillusioned or to have an immature mind, but what kids understand—and some adults have forgotten—is imagination represents possibility, and possibility is the key ingredient to making something real. If you can think it up, you can figure out a way to make it happen.

Is it possible to let your imagination get out of hand? Sure. Can it cause you to lose touch with reality? You bet. But in the long run, the risk is more than worth the reward. To give up your imagination is to give up a piece of you. It's not just any piece, either. It's the piece that really knows how to live. It's what lets you find joy in the unpleasant and what allows you to believe in miracles. Put it to work, because if you don't it will most certainly leave...and getting it back is hard.

#51
If you must compare, compare yourself to the you of yesterday, not to anybody else.

I know it's tempting to look at other people and want what they have. Maybe the competitive juices in you start flowing and you get angry or frustrated that you aren't at their level. Whether it's your finances, talents or opportunities that you are looking to improve, don't be upset by what others have and you don't. There could be many reasons why they are in a better situation than you or more talented than you. It doesn't mean you can't get to their level, but obsessing about them is a distraction. It wastes time and energy. Instead, focus on yourself and how *you* can improve. Let their success motivate you (or even be the example you model), but don't let it consume you. And definitely don't let it change you. If you feel the need to compare yourself to someone, compare your-self to the person you were yesterday. Identify where you can im-prove, and then, at the end of every day, ask yourself: *"Did I get better today?"*

If you take just one step in the right direction every day—no matter how small—over time those tiny steps will add up, and be-fore you know it you'll be a changed person. You will be better than before. You may have even caught up to your competition. But, whether you have or not, the real competition should be with yourself. How much better can *you* get? How great can *you* be? Worry less about being *the* best and more about being *your* best. Focus on *your* effort and *your* hard work, because that is what you can improve. All that other stuff is beyond your control and should, therefore, be beyond your consideration. Remove it from your radar. When you do that, everything else will take care of it-self.

That's not to say there's no room for competition. There is certainly a time and place for it. In many ways, competition can be great because it tends to bring out our best effort. It's our competi-tive spirit that encourages us to try harder and push longer, and the desire to defeat our opponent is the great motivator. You should always want to win, and try your hardest to do so. There's nothing wrong with that. Competition builds character. It teaches you how to persevere and push through challenges. There are many other things to be gained from it, too, but none of those benefits should come at the expense of your integrity, your honor, or your self-respect. Don't sacrifice being a good person for the temptations that competition sometimes presents. You may win now, but in the long run you are hurting yourself and setting up for a big fall. Yes, there are areas of life where success is determined mostly by how often you win, and it's hard to be successful if you don't earn a few victories at least, but if it requires you to compromise your values, it's not worth it.

Most importantly, try to keep things in perspective. Don't let your shortcomings discourage you from improving. Don't let your talents make you complacent. You know yourself better than anyone else. You know when you've really given your best effort, or if you've slacked off. Deep down, you know if you've done the all things you need to do to get better. So be honest with yourself. Know who you are, and who you want to be, and then do what it takes to get there. Let *your* progress be your measuring stick. If you are better today than you were yesterday, you're off to a good start.

#50

If you're going to put your name on it, make sure it's work you can be proud of.

Whether you're working on a big, newsworthy project or a simple, routine task, take pride in your work. What you do—big or small—becomes part of your legacy, and you want it to be one that has substance and value. Not only will you be remembered for what you do, but also for the way you do it. Do it the right way— by paying attention to detail and giving your best effort. Anything less than that, no matter how unimportant the task may seem, is selling yourself short. Set a standard of excellence and do everything you can to meet that standard in every project you take on. Doing so will demonstrate to others that you are someone who can be depended on produce high quality work.

You don't build a reputation like this by giving great effort once in a while, or by trying hard most of the time. This kind of thing takes time to develop. It has to be proven over a series of tasks. Taking pride in your work is more than just a good habit. It's a way of life, something that you must buy into completely or it loses its effect. People don't endorse the guy who tries hard only occasionally, or when it's convenient for him. They want to work with someone who will do his absolute best, every time.

There's another reason—beyond dependability and high standards—why it's so important that you always give your best effort. That reason is respect. Respect for those that come into contact with your work. Respect for your name and your family. Most importantly, it's about having respect for yourself. All those other things are great, and important in their own way, but if you don't have enough respect for yourself to *want* to give it your all, then we have bigger problems to address. The greatest rewards come when you show others that you are committed and that you value your reputation. Others won't respect you until you respect yourself.

Being respected by your peers is one of the best compliments you can receive. It means that people who are in the same line of work, those who best understand the challenges and difficulties you face, admire what you've been able to do. This isn't something to disregard. It's a sign that you're doing things right. Respect isn't something that you can demand from others, and it's not something you are entitled to. You must earn it—every day, little by little, in everything that you do. It will grow over time, but it starts with one simple rule: If you're going to put your name on something, make sure it's work you can be proud of.

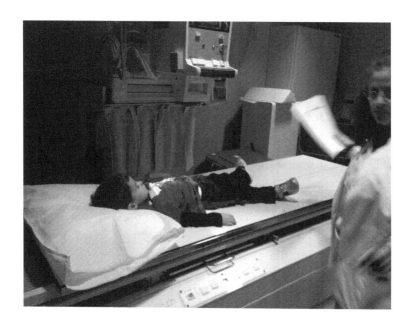

#49

Being fearless is not the same as being brave.

There is a big difference between being fearless and being brave. When you're brave, you have courage in the face of fear. You are aware of the possible dangers, yet you push on in spite of them. Maybe it's for a noble cause. Maybe it's because you're foolish. Maybe it's because you don't know what else to do. No matter the reason, bravery often leads to a calculated risk. You know it could turn out badly, but to you the risk is not nearly as great as the potential reward. Some may disagree, but I think bravery is admirable. It's a willingness to put something on the line, because you truly believe someone—maybe another person, maybe you, maybe both—stands to gain significantly from it. It's action for the greater good. That's not a bad quality to have in yourself, nor to find in someone else.

When you are fearless, you don't think about consequences or risk. You aren't acting nobly, you're acting dangerously. You might attack the situation head on, but if you aren't careful, you could find yourself in trouble. Without a plan, and without proper respect for the danger, you expose yourself to unnecessary risk. You might put others in danger as well. It's like the cocky cowboy gunslinger that walks into town and just starts shooting everything up. Sooner or later he's going to walk into the wrong town and meet his match. Acting fearlessly will catch up to you if you aren't careful. Being "careful" means being aware of what's at stake and acknowledging the challenge before you. It doesn't mean you shouldn't eventually continue on bravely, but first have a plan.

There is no shame in being afraid of something. Don't be embarrassed by it. If anything, fear is a sign of intelligence. It's a warning that there is potential danger looming. Fear is an instinct that's lasted through many centuries of evolution. Don't hide from it. Don't ignore it. Listen to it. Learn from it. And then see if there's a way you can overcome it. Often, overcoming fear is just a matter of asking yourself what the worst-case scenario is should you fail. Many times the fear turns out to be unwarranted. Sometimes it's legitimate. In either situation, you must decide if you think the risk is worth what you are trying to achieve. If it is, then that's when it's time to be brave.

Determining when to be brave and when to move on is tricky. Ultimately, it boils down to deciding what's important to you. Your values and your priorities will make it pretty easy to establish what you think is worth fighting for. It's important that you have some way of deciding this, because you have to choose your battles. Taking on every challenge and every cause will leave you exhausted.

You won't have the time or resources to attack them all bravely and with the proper attention. This will cloud your priorities and could lead to fearless behavior. If all else fails, listen to your heart. Fight for what's important to you. Acknowledge your fear and push through it. Most of all, don't be afraid to be brave.

#48

Some people will do anything to distract you from your goals; don't let it happen.

Throughout your life, it's inevitable that you will encounter a certain type of person. The more you achieve, the more of them you'll meet. These people aren't going to help you do well. They are jealous. They are lazy or beaten down—some are hateful and merciless. They've long ago given up on their own dreams, and therefore don't like the idea of anyone else having them, either. At best, they'll be indifferent to what you do, but at their worst they will do whatever they can to yank you into their misery. If they can't be happy, why should you? It's sad to think that you, or anyone else, will have to navigate through pessimism and jealousy, but it's real, so you should be prepared for it. I think it's important you are aware that it's out there, and that you know how you'll respond, but never, ever let them get ahold of you.

You can't control the way others think or how they act. But you can control how it affects you. When a negative-thinking person tries to bring you down, there are a few ways to respond. You can listen to them. This is almost always wrong. Rarely does this kind of person have any intention of doing anything to help you. They may try to be nice, but their negativity will show through. They aren't rooting for you. They can barely root for themselves. Another option is to ignore them. This is safe and effective. It won't hurt you, but it won't do much to make you better, either. A third choice is to use their doubt as motivation. Let it inspire you to prove them wrong. It's hard to avoid hearing the criticism, which is why it's so beneficial to learn how to let it energize you. You don't have to actually respond to them. Let your success be the reply.

Even though it's a long shot to work, you might feel the urge to help these people change their attitudes. It's not a bad idea to give it a try. It's not always clear how someone gets to a point where they've lost hope, but sometimes they are the victims of bad break after bad break. What's happened to them might not be their fault. Still, they can decide how to react to those misfortunes, and with your help maybe they can change. With your encouragement, things may start to get better for them.

I don't want to make it sound like everyone is out to get you, or that you are the only person doing anything worthwhile. Those who do things to interrupt your success—whether purposefully or unknowingly—are in the minority. More often than not, people will be quick to lend a hand or give an encouraging word. That makes it even more tragic to let the few dictate your behavior. Surround yourself with people who will challenge and encourage you.

Find people who inspire you. Make friends with those who are already where you want to be. Stay confident. Work hard. And, no matter how good or bad things may be, don't let someone else bring you down.

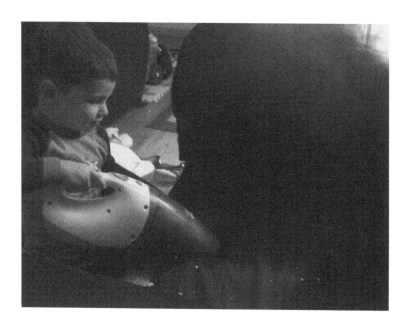

#47

The man's role is to ignore the stereotypes and do whatever needs to be done.

The man's role is to ignore the stereotypes and do whatever needs to be done. Read that sentence again: The man's role is to ignore the stereotypes and do whatever needs to be done. I don't care what anyone else ever tries to tell you about it, this is all you need to know. The idea that certain chores are "a man's job" or "the woman's responsibility" is ancient. Not only is this way of thinking patronizing and backwards, it's inaccurate. There is no doubt, gender stereotypes run deep. In some way, they are present in just about everything that we do, but that doesn't mean we have to recognize or follow them. The moment you start labeling tasks based on gender you set our evolution back. You promote close-mindedness. You come off as chauvinistic. Plus, it's a good way to end up on the couch. Does it bother you that only *men* seem to get sent to sleep on the couch? Good, maybe *now* you get the point.

When you're older and have a family of your own, you and your wife may get in a pattern where you each take on certain tasks as part of your regular routine, and that's fine. Maybe you each are better at or more comfortable doing one thing versus another. I have no problem with that. It's a smart and effective use of your time and talents. But things aren't always that simple. Sometimes schedules change. Sometimes extenuating circumstances get in the way. Sometimes the kids insist on Daddy giving them a bath. Don't forget that you are more than capable of doing all the things she normally does, just as she is capable of doing any of your tasks. So when the need arises, step up and fill in. It's not enough that you are each able to do those things, you must be ready and willing to do them when necessary.

Whether it's at home or somewhere else, everyone benefits when you are eager to take on any and all tasks. When you are that person it helps to send a message to everyone else—first, that you aren't too good to help in any way possible; and second, it encourages them to participate, too. There's no better way to gain the support of others than to set the example yourself. And the best example you can set is one of selflessness. It applies everywhere, but it's crucial you at least do it at home. If you won't help your family at all costs, how can you expect to bring value anywhere else?

Being part of a family is like being on a team. It's the most important team you'll be a member of. When that operation runs smoothly, the other parts of your life are more likely to follow. This means if you notice that a load of laundry needs to be done, do it. Dishes are in the sink? Wash them. Do whatever you can, whenever and however you can, to make sure your team is functioning as efficiently as possible. Want to talk about roles? That's your role. To do whatever needs to be done. Period.

#46

Manners are typically only noticed when they're lacking. Don't get noticed.

Back when I was little, I remember my parents telling me about a compliment they received for raising polite children. They were proud of the way your uncle and I represented our family, and were flattered that someone recognized it. At the time it didn't mean much to me, but now, having children of my own, I understand exactly how they felt. Manners *matter*. They aren't just something parents push their kids to learn because they have nothing better to do. Having them demonstrates—and earns—respect. Manners are a reflection of your upbringing. They're a reflection of *you.*

Most of the time, we go about our day not really paying attention to how friendly or polite other people are. Occasionally, you may notice someone who is extra nice or who offers an unsolicited smile, but typically it doesn't register with us. Maybe it's because we're so focused on what we have going on that we aren't paying attention. Or maybe it's because we just expect people to treat others with respect and don't feel compelled to make a big deal when someone does things they *should* be doing. No matter what the reasons are—whether you notice well-mannered people or not—one thing is for sure: You *will* notice someone who is rude. When people have no manners they stand out. Not only are they difficult to be around or work with, their behavior can ruin your day. Whether they actually do or not is up to you, but it will certainly be difficult to ignore their rudeness.

Even though good manners are often overlooked, it's still not an excuse for lacking them. I'd much rather you blend in with all the other polite people than have a reputation as the rude guy. Everything is better when we are nice to each other. Things go more smoothly, people are happier and more seems to get done. This isn't a coincidence. It's the collective attitude that determines how things operate, and the better the atmosphere, the better the results. It may seem like a stretch, but just being nice to others can help create that mood. Do what you can to make your surroundings as conducive to success as possible.

As your dad, I am so proud when someone compliments your mom and me on your behavior. Being well-mannered is about the simplest, yet most impactful trait you can have. When you have a reputation for being polite—when you're well-liked—opportunities are more likely to pop up. And, even though being nice won't always be enough to get you in the door, being rude is a sure way to have that door slammed in your face.

#45

Magic is all around you, if you choose to see it.

Magic is for real. It exists everywhere and in everything. And if you know what you're looking for and how to find it, it's not hard to see. Children are really good at this. They see magic all around them and they are amazed by it. It inspires them and expands their minds. It makes them believe the unbelievable. They live life in awe of just about everything. It's like they're seeing something beautiful for the first time—and, in many cases, it's because they are. For kids, it's not about whether the magic is real, it's about when and where it's going to show up again. And it will continue to show up, and continue to amaze them, for as long as they let it.

Eventually, though, they begin to grow up. They get busy. The moments become less frequent and the awe just isn't as breathtaking. Other things take their attention away from the tiny miracles around them. Stuff just doesn't seem as amazing anymore. And before long, they forget how to see the magic at all. Life becomes a mess of responsibilities—a slate of duties that leaves no time for sunsets and fireworks. It's not the magic that goes away, it's the imagination—the wonder—that leaves. It's not the world that changes, it's the person. But it doesn't have to be that way. If you want the magic to stay with you, all you have to do is refuse to stop believing in it.

Believing in magic is not something that's only for kids. It's just that they're the ones that are most likely to do so. Somewhere along the line—in addition to letting themselves go through the motions of life—adults get this crazy idea that magic is silly, that it's just a trick and there's nothing special about it. They become convinced that it's children's make believe, and nothing more. That's simply not true. You can find something magical everywhere you look. Miracles surround us, and new ones occur every day, but our eyes will only see what our heart is willing to feel.

Life can be hard, but don't let it turn you cold. When you limp through it, you miss all the magic. Live with open eyes and an open mind. See the magic before you. Let it take you by the hand and show you all the beauty you'd otherwise overlook. No matter how old you are, always try to see the world through the eyes of an amazed young child, the one who only knows life to be one fascination after another. Magic is all around you, but you have to want to see it.

#44

All that really matters is whether you are naughty or nice.

We can spend time making life really complicated, trying to figure out what fancy toy will make our days easier or our interactions more pleasant—and there are plenty of good options—but the best answer, the most effective one, is also probably the simplest: Be nice to others. It's as simple as that. Will it solve all of our problems? No. But it will certainly give us a head start toward happier days. It's one of the first things you learn in school and for good reason—it's one of the most important. No matter how old you get and no matter where you go, the importance of being nice to others does not change. It is, and always will be, the right thing to do. Still, it's surprising to see how many of us forget this lesson.

Knowing how to be nice and actually doing it are two different things. You could be having a bad day. Or someone else may antagonize you. You may even feel like they're *trying* to get this kind of reaction from you. You will probably have the urge to fight back; you may want to tell them how you feel about their lousy attitude. Resist the urge. Most of the time this won't accomplish anything. No matter how upset you are, and no matter how deserving they may be, it's almost always not worth it.

If you think about any of the great problems we face, nearly all of them could be improved if only everyone involved followed this one simple rule: Just be nice. Think of others often—if not always—and do what you can to make their lives better. It doesn't have to be a world-changing idea or action, either. Sometimes your impact can be felt with something as simple as a smile toward a stranger. They feel better, you feel better, and for the rest of the day—maybe longer—anyone else you meet will feel the effects. Sure, you may not always be treated this way by others. So what? Be nice to them anyway. Don't let their attitude affect yours.

You can accomplish all sorts of things in your life. You can amass tons of wealth, win distinguished awards and earn amazing accolades. While they are all great—and can lead to a fulfilling and successful life—when you're dead and gone those things all become footnotes. They're not what people remember you for. They're not what makes you admirable. They're not the reasons people love you when you're living, either. Not by themselves, anyway. What stands out about a person—when they're alive as well as when they're gone—isn't their money, awards, or achievements. What stands out is how they've treated others and the impression that they've made. Rich or poor, known or unknown, when all the junk is pushed aside and the quality of a man is measured, the size of his wallet is nothing compared to the size of his heart. All that really matters is whether you are naughty or nice.

#43

**Develop an internal soundtrack to your life.
Shuffle the songs in your head
as you need them.**

There is a song for every situation. Everything you experience—everything you *feel*—has probably been explained to some degree in a song. That's good for two reasons. First, it lets you know you're not alone. Whether you're at a high or low point in your life, someone else has been there, too. It can keep you energized and motivated to continue working hard, or it can give you hope and remind you there are better days ahead. Second, it can be excellent therapy. Music is a great healer. It will walk with you during sad times, keeping you company while you process difficult feelings. Music is powerful, it's diverse, and it's at your disposal. Use it to your advantage.

I have less than zero musical talent. I'm ashamed to admit that I also have a rather poor knowledge base when it comes to music—things like which artist sang which song—but I know a song that resonates with me when I hear it. It could be the hook, or one lyric or just the beat that gets me. But if I'm feeling a certain way when a song that moves me is played, the effects of the feeling grow stronger. Music evokes emotion. It stirs memories we've long forgotten. Sometimes it's just flat out entertaining. It can serve any purpose you want. The key is to figure out how you can put it to use. How can it help *you?*

For some of our more talented friends, creating music is one way to take advantage of its power. You don't have to be a musical genius to reap the emotional benefits that making music can provide, although it helps. Especially if you ever want anyone to listen to it. Still, the act of making music or writing lyrics will help you work through your thoughts. Just like any other creative outlet, it provides a release that we all need from time to time. Even if you're like me, and barely know which end of a trumpet to blow into, music can still make an impact on you. Luckily, many talented people continue to do the hard work for us. All we have to do is listen.

When you hear songs that strike a chord with you (pun alert), store them away. Make a mental note of which songs had which effects on you and under which circumstances. If they were helpful in any way, those are the songs you want to rely on when you find yourself in that situation again. Make a playlist or just add them to your internal soundtrack. Then, shuffle the songs around in your head as you need them. Feeling awesome? Maybe that's when the Superman theme song kicks on in your mind. It may sound crazy, but when you associate songs with situations or feelings, it gives you the calm of having been there before. You already know what to do. The song is just there to remind you to smile through it.

#42

What's funny to you may be offensive to others.

Having a sense of humor is important. It's fun to joke around. It's good to share a laugh. But the key is that the laugh is *shared*. Always keep in mind that what's funny to you might be offensive to others. If you think something you say will upset someone else—even if you mean no offense by it—it's probably a good idea to stay away. Don't say it. A joke is not funny when it's at the expense of someone who doesn't appreciate it or is offended by it. Not only that, but it can make you look insensitive, classless and rude. Does this mean you may miss an opportunity to make some people laugh? Yes, but I'd rather you miss a hundred opportunities like that than upset or offend someone else. When in doubt, keep it to yourself.

With all of that said, it's not always your responsibility to protect others—especially from the truth. Off-color jokes and rude comments are one thing, but sometimes people need to thicken their skin when it comes to criticism or a little needling. This is a good habit to adopt yourself, as well. Don't take these kinds of things personally. If you really do find yourself upset or offended it's okay to speak up, but make sure that before you do you look at the comments objectively. Are you being too sensitive or did that person really cross a line? Of course you should defend yourself, your family, and anyone else who is wrongfully attacked, but don't jump the gun. It's okay to be the punch line of a joke every once in a while. If you can't laugh at yourself, who can you laugh at?

For many jokes and comments, there is a time and a place. You can avoid awkward or hostile exchanges if you have some sort of judgment when it comes to when and where you direct your humor. It doesn't take a professional stand-up comedian to know when that is, either. All you need is a little common sense. And, again, if you're not sure how it will be taken, assume the worst and stay quiet. This can all get a little confusing if someone gets offended by a comment you thought was harmless. Even if you try to put yourself in their shoes, and look at it from their perspective, you still may not see why it would bother them. Then, sure enough, as soon as you blast off your one-liner they take it to heart. You can't always predict the reaction you'll get, and you may be wrong when you try to guess. Sometimes mistakes happen. And it's not the end of the world when they do. It might be embarrassing and it might cause some drama in your relationship, but if this happens to you, apologize for what you said. Don't make excuses. Don't deflect the blame. *Definitely*, don't downplay their hurt. Just apologize. They may have overreacted. They may have misunderstood you. It doesn't matter. If things are going to be put back to normal, you have only one option. Say you're sorry.

All of the concern over whether or not you're going to offend someone might make you want to avoid being funny altogether. Please don't let it make you gun-shy. Laughter is a really big part of having fun and enjoying ourselves. It's hard to be in a bad mood when you're laughing. We need it to get through the monotony of our days, and to bring some light into our lives. It brings us closer together and helps to create memories. Humor has a very big place in a happy life. The challenge, sometimes, is in finding that place, and not upsetting others in the meantime.

#41

You can be anything you choose to be.
Choose to be amazing.

From the time you're very little, people will ask—and you'll try to answer—one very important question: What do you want to be? They might be referring to your career goals, but maybe not. Maybe they're asking a much deeper question—one that I hope you ask yourself often as you grow up. You can "be" anything you choose, but what is it you really *want?* Do you want to be someone who floats through life, going through the motions and barely leaving a footprint anywhere? Or do you want to be someone that makes an impact on the world? No matter what career you choose, as a person you can be ordinary or amazing. Why not choose amazing?

All that separates an ordinary person from someone who makes their mark is a willingness to go a little bit further, a desire to be special. They say the last mile is never crowded, and it's true. Not everyone has the drive or the commitment to see it through. But the ones that do are rewarded for it. They get to experience life the way we're supposed to—with happiness and fulfillment. It's not the easiest route to take, and it requires effort every day, but I really believe that's how we were meant to exist. You might find happiness some days or in some areas of your life, but until you find a way to do what fulfills you, there will always be something missing.

That's not to say you need a flashy lifestyle to be amazing. Some of the most extraordinary people come from ordinary walks of life, but they are able to impact others in a meaningful way. They aren't any less amazing just because you've never heard of them. In a way, those people are even more amazing, because the things they do don't bring them fame or fortune. Still, their actions are powerful, making a difference for someone, somewhere. What you actually do is not nearly as important as the commitment to do it as well as you can. An amazing person is the one that gets the absolute most out of his abilities, no matter how minimal or expansive his talents are.

There might be some days when you're beaten down and find yourself fighting just to get by. At times like that you may doubt that you ever had, or ever will have, the ability to decide the path your life is going to take. You may see it as something that was fun to imagine when you were young, but is simply not realistic as an adult. It's a common thought, but it's simply not true. That belief is the barrier all amazing people have to break through at one point or another. There will be doubts. There will be difficulty. There will be disappointments. It's challenging to be amazing, but that's what makes it great. If it wasn't hard, everyone would do it. Many things will stand in your way, but when you push through them the rewards are worth it. You can be anything you choose to be. No matter what you choose, don't settle for anything less than amazing.

#40

They say, "Don't ever meet your hero." I say, "Make your hero someone worth meeting."

It's great to have heroes. They are someone to look up to, to motivate you and to model yourself after. They are the inspiration for childhood dreams. They are living proof that anything is possible—that if you can dream it, you can do it. They have dreamt it. They have done it. And if they can do it, then so can you. There's a reason why we look up to them. They, at least in some small way, represent the person we want to become. There's nothing wrong with admiring someone who has accomplished the same goals and lived the same dreams as you have for yourself. Just be careful that you don't turn them into someone they're not, because, if you do, they *will* disappoint you.

It's been said that you should never meet your hero, for fear that he won't be the person you grew to admire, or that maybe she'll do something to let you down. What would happen if a thing they did or said made you realize they weren't someone worthy of your admiration? Would you be crushed to find out that your hero was a jerk? That he or she wasn't like the character they played in the movies? Or that they are rude to others when there aren't cameras pointed at them? It's a fair concern. No one wants to be disappointed in someone they look up to. We all want our heroes to be as magnificent in real life as they are on the big screen. But when you build heroes up, putting them on pedestals as high as those we create for them, it's very difficult to live up to the expectations. Chances are they're going to fall at least a little short. They're human, after all. That's why it's so important to be careful who you choose to look up to.

A hero doesn't have to be famous. They don't have to be a movie star, musician or athlete. What they should be is a person of high character, who has integrity and a track record of doing good. They should have the qualities you'd like to have, and the talents you want to develop—or those you can appreciate, at least. Sometimes it's easy to forget that heroes are people, too. Even the best ones make mistakes once in a while. It might be disappointing when they do, but that doesn't mean they aren't worthy of your admiration. You can learn a lot from the way they handle their mistakes—maybe more than you can from their successes. Are they honest? Apologetic? Committed to fixing wrongs and doing right? Don't make your hero someone who never makes mistakes; choose someone who's not afraid to admit his shortcomings, someone who uses his weaknesses as an opportunity to get even better.

When you find yourself admiring a person, especially someone you've never met before, ask yourself why you admire them. Are you infatuated with their fame or their talents? Or is there more to them than that? What have they *really* done to earn your admiration? Start with high standards for the person you choose to look up to. Don't fall in line, idolizing the latest trendy star. Find someone that resonates with you—someone *you* can relate to. Most importantly, find someone who stands for something they believe in, who is not concerned with what others think, and is brave enough to follow their own convictions. When you discover the person who connects with you in all of those ways, *that's* when you've found someone hero-worthy. And if you're ever lucky enough to meet that person, not only will they not let you down, you might be surprised how much more they'll bring you up.

#39
Your princess is out there.
You'll find her when the time is right.

Call me a romantic, but I do think fate plays a part in finding the person you were meant to be with. In my mind, there are too many variables to believe anything else. Still, I was fortunate to end up with your mom. Fate may have introduced us, but without a little bit of luck, there's no way things would have worked out the way they did. I really believe that there is someone for everyone, and, even though she may have settled on me, your mom is definitely *my* princess. So yes, we're lucky to have met. We're fortunate that we are happy together and that we have great kids to show for it. But, in my opinion, fate played a big part in it all working out. As it will with you.

Love cannot be forced. You can be on the lookout for it and hopeful that it will find you, but if you try forcing it when it's not there, things won't turn out well. You might notice all your buddies starting to get married, and you might start to feel some pressure—perhaps even panic—that you are never going to have that yourself. Neither pressure nor panic will help you feel any better. Instead, remain open to the idea, but don't let it dictate your decisions. Find the middle ground between being vulnerable and not getting hurt. Open your heart, but don't let just anyone fill it. Simply put: live your life and let love find you. Then, when it does, don't ignore it.

You'll know when you've found her. Things will feel different. Even the dullest moments will have a shine around them because you've got her. If you're lucky enough to find yourself in that situation, embrace it! Let it happen, because those moments are fleeting. When you stall, or think too much, the moment might pass you by. Whether or not a relationship is successful in the long run depends greatly on timing. *When* you find her is almost as important as who she is. If the timing is off—if you're not ready or if she's distracted—then even the matches made in heaven may struggle.

Know that somewhere out there is the person you're meant to be with. They are going about their life wondering who you are and when they'll find you. And, in the meantime, you might be doing the same. It's fine to think about this and imagine the family you'll one day have, just don't let it consume you. Don't spend all your time preoccupied with whether you'll ever find the right person for you. You may end up overlooking what's right beneath your nose. You could miss life as it's happening. Put yourself out there, but then let love come to you. Give it a chance, but don't force it. Keep the faith that your princess is out there, and trust that you'll find her when the time is right.

#38
Know how to lead, know when to follow.

The world needs leaders. We need someone who is going to step up, take charge, and show us how to get things done. We need someone to lead us through crisis and hardship, someone to inspire us to improve our surroundings. We need a leader who is motivated to help the greater good, and who thinks about himself only after others are taken care of. There are plenty of people out there who fit these descriptions and many are already leading us to better days. But that doesn't mean there's not room for one more. Be the leader others are looking for. Stand up for the things you believe in, and encourage people to follow you toward protecting those beliefs. The world needs someone that inspires change, someone that becomes the example to follow, and there's no reason that "someone" can't be you.

Fear might be one of the biggest reasons you hesitate to lead. You may worry what others will think. You might be concerned that no one will follow you. You could be afraid you'll fail. So what? Put yourself out there anyway. Life is too short, and the window to make an impact is too small, to let fear or doubt creep in. Once you've experienced failure, you realize it's not the worst thing in the world. You will also realize that you stand to gain much more if you're successful than you will lose if you're not. All it takes is dedication to the cause and a little support to start, and you can make unbelievable progress. The key to being a great leader is as much the courage to get started as it is the skill to lead.

The ability to lead is important for many reasons, but maybe just as important is recognizing when to step back and allow yourself to be led by others. When too many opinions are involved, decision-making gets jammed up and progress stalls. Leadership is about improving a situation, not adding to the confusion. If you are in an environment that is under control, and those involved (including you) are satisfied with the leadership and direction, that's a cue that you may want to stay out of the way. Even if you think you could do a better job, it's not always a good idea to interfere. There are times when even the best leaders need to fall in line behind someone else.

Whether you are a powerful leader, or among a large group of followers, you still have the opportunity to lead by example. Sometimes you can set the tone even more strongly than the actual leader by following them and encouraging others to do so as well. You often don't even need to say anything. Your actions alone will be enough to gain their following—especially if you've already earned their respect. A great leader isn't someone who barks their orders the loudest or makes people fear them. A great leader is someone who is capable and ready to lead, when and however needed. They are someone who inspires. They also recognize when to take a step back and let another leader direct them. They know *how* to lead, but they also know *when* to follow.

#37

New beginnings are the same as old endings,
until you change something.

We all have something about ourselves that we'd like to change, some physical feature or habit that holds us back from becoming the person we know we can become. So we set goals, make resolutions and devise plans to make a change. Those are all good ideas and part of the process, but they are only *part* of the process. All too often we identify where we want to improve and how, and then we stop there. We might tell a few people about it, but nothing more. That's not enough. Talking about how you want to improve is one thing, but nothing will change unless you actually make the effort. Until you bring them to life, plans are nothing more than great ideas. They're just a bunch of talk.

The idea that we can create for ourselves a fresh start—a new beginning—is an intriguing one. It's encouraging. It's empowering. It makes us feel like we are in control of our lives. And we are. But it's up to *you* to claim control over which direction your life takes. If you don't, you'll fall right back in line, going through the motions and waiting for something or someone to make a decision for you. Most of the time, when you leave it up to others, not much will happen. They are going through their own challenges and their own struggles. They don't have time to even think about helping you get yourself right. If you are going to see those big plans become reality, *you* have to make them so. You might get a little boost here or there, but the real effort has to be yours.

Getting better is hard work. The process—the *grind*—of improving is where the real challenge lies. Not because what you're trying to do is difficult, necessarily, but because it takes discipline and commitment to continue on—especially when the rewards are far off in the distance. Recognition and praise often comes long after the hard work has been put in. And the work is mostly done when others aren't there to encourage you. You will feel like you are alone. You will question if it's even worth it. You will want to quit many times before you reach the end. But you can't. Because if you let yourself quit once, it will be easy to do it again. Fight through the temptation to give up. You have to want the change badly enough to be your own motivation. It requires a little faith that the rewards will be worth the effort, but they will be.

We have an ongoing opportunity to make changes, to improve ourselves and our circumstances in life. It's never too late to take a shot at something you've always wanted to do or become. So do it. Drop the excuses and do it now. Embrace the grind and test your limits. Self-improvement is a process, an evolution (one that never stops), and the desire to explore its boundaries should not be ignored. As you grow and progress you'll have to leave comfort zones to explore new frontiers. You'll have to bravely take on new challenges. But first, you have to initiate growth. Only you can take the first step. Until you do, new beginnings are nothing more than old endings. Don't settle for that. Go out and make a change.

#36

Effort + Determination = Success. Period.

Everyone wants to be considered successful. Determining your definition of success is half the battle, but even those who know their ultimate goals sometimes struggle with how to get there. The formula for success can seem so complicated and overwhelming, but really it's quite simple: Effort plus determination equals success. The concept is simple—it's the execution that takes some work. But if you want something badly enough, and you put in the necessary time and effort, eventually you will achieve it. It might take a while, and it might not be in exactly the way you were hoping, but there will be a payoff. Your hard work will be proven worthwhile. The question isn't whether you *can* do something; it's whether you have the commitment to stick with it until you do. With enough fortitude, anything is possible.

It's common to see someone who has become successful and assume that success came overnight—that they were chosen at random or were just in the right place at the right time. Lucky them! But the truth is, hardly any great achievement *ever* came suddenly or without hard work. Success is the culmination of small victories over time, and almost all of those victories are earned by first overcoming a series of failures. The polished, successful person you admire has most likely failed over and over again long before reaching the pinnacle you found them at. What separates them from all the others isn't talent as much as perseverance. They have learned to treat their setbacks like the building blocks that they are, and even though they may get discouraged too, they don't let it derail them.

When the frustrations start piling up, you might begin to wonder why you are putting yourself through it all. There is no single answer that will always be right. Each situation is different, but it all comes back to one simple question. If you can answer it, you can decide if you should continue pushing ahead. The question is: *How badly do you want it?* If you want to overcome a specific challenge you are facing or achieve a certain goal you've set more than you are bothered by the setbacks, it will be easy to justify continuing on. But if you're not determined enough—if you don't want it badly enough—then you're missing a key piece of the success formula. If you are ever going to reach that goal, you need to find the motivation to persevere.

Even though we know what it takes to be successful, we can never be sure when exactly that success will break through. Because it's so uncertain, the best way I've found to stay sane while plugging away is to find joy in the process. Embrace it. Embrace *all* of it, too. The person that puts extra effort into the parts that are least enjoyable will usually be the one that stands out. Everyone wants to do the fun stuff. Those parts are easy. But if you commit to always giving everything you have—your best effort and your highest enthusiasm—to all pieces of the puzzle, the success formula will work.

#35
The dreamers of the day are dangerous men.

There's nothing wrong with letting your imagination run wild and coming up with some big ideas. In fact, I want you to do that. I want you to dream big dreams and create fantastic thoughts. I want you to imagine a world that's ideal for you, enjoying a life you are proud of. In order for any these wishes to come true, they have to begin as fantasy. They have to start as nothing more than visions, hopes and dreams. But they can't stay that way. If they are ever going to become real, you have to take action. You have to put in the necessary work and breathe life into them. Many, many wonderful dreams die because no one is there to nurture them. They live inside the person's head until, eventually, the effects of inaction start to write over them, and before long they disappear.

Don't let that happen to you. Dream with an intention to bring them to life. Dream with your eyes open.

The people who dream with their eyes open—the dreamers of the day—are the ones most likely to make them become real. They form dreams with the understanding that they are a destination—a place the person actually intends to get to. As ambitious and unlikely as their fantasies may seem, they never label them impossible and they rarely question whether they'll achieve them. Coming up short is simply *not* an option. They are dangerous—not to themselves or to others but—to the school of thought that there are limitations to our potential. They are dangerous because they make things happen. They stretch expectations and belief structures to their breaking points. They challenge others to be better. They shatter doubt and fear. They prove that any*thing* is possible and that any*one* can do it. And, in the process, they inspire us to do the same.

One of the saddest things in life is hearing the regrets people have about not taking a chance—about how they were too scared, or too cautious, to chase their dreams. The people who "dream by night" do it in the safety of their own minds, without a willingness to take risks. Fear forces them into taking the safe route, where they fall in line with everyone else, never choosing to stick their neck out. Then, one day, they finally "wake up" and are hit with the gravity of the opportunity that was missed. You rarely get a second chance to take a shot at those goals you set aside, to follow your heart and search for true happiness. The greatest punishment anyone can be dealt is to wonder what might have been. It's not something to leave to chance. Take a shot. Do it now, while the opportunity is there. Try something you want to try, no matter how unlikely it might be to work out. Feed your soul while you can, because we only live once. Regret on your deathbed is not something you want to experience.

When it comes to the dreams that you create, live for yourself. Your dreams should be your own. Don't let me, or anyone else, talk you out of them or into others. Create the life you want. Only you can decide what makes you happy, and only you knows what it will take. Ultimately, the destination is up to you, but there's only one way to get there. Be dangerous. Be a day dreamer.

#34
Freedom is a right not to be taken lightly. Execute, but don't abuse.

As you grow and experience more, I hope you'll come to understand how fortunate you are to have the freedoms you have. Even though *we* believe it's the right of all to be free, not everyone is. For us, it's a right that we're entitled to, but it wasn't always that way. And, in some parts of the world it still isn't. You have the ability to spend each day doing whatever you want (as long as it's within the law), and that is a privilege not to be taken for granted. Many people died fighting to earn those rights for you, and it's an everyday struggle to maintain them. Knowing about your freedoms is not enough; they're something you should take advantage of as well.

When I say take advantage of your freedoms, I don't mean abuse them. I mean put them to use. Vote when you have the chance. Travel to different places. Choose a career that makes you happy. The course your life takes is entirely up to you and within your control. Sometimes it's scary to think about it like that, because that's a lot of pressure to put on yourself. But really, would you want it any other way? When you call the shots, the responsibility is on you to make it work, but you also don't have as many hurdles to jump over. With this model, *you* are your biggest obstacle. Sure, things could be better than they are. We do have some flawed systems. But *nothing* is ever really perfect. And, despite the imperfections, there are certainly more than enough opportunities for you to find happiness. You have the right to enjoy life.

It's natural, when we are afforded a little space, to try to test its limits. Just like a child checking to see how much he or she can get away with, we push the boundaries of our freedoms. This can slowly lead to exploitation, and before long the rights are abused. Unfortunately, when abuse takes place, those who afford the freedoms—whether it's parents toward their children or a government toward its population—tend to have a knee-jerk reaction, and they pull back the reigns even further than before. Trust becomes an issue, and any progress is damaged if not lost. At that point, there is even more ground to make up just to get back to where you were.

The opportunity to control your own destiny and create the life you want is a wonderful thing. It might be the greatest thing. For those that subscribe to the theory of Carpe Diem, this is what it's all about. You have been given permission to seize the day and to make it your own. The means to attack life are at your disposal. You are free to live as you wish. As a result, you owe it to yourself to settle for nothing less than what makes you happy. This means putting those freedoms to good use. It means maximizing your opportunities and it means doing so in a way that does not exploit those privileges. Freedom is a right not to be taken lightly. It can be taken from you as quickly as it's given. Execute, but don't abuse.

#33

Be the light that brightens up another's day.

I think general kindness is one of the things that gets lost in the busy lives we lead. We become so preoccupied with ourselves, we forget that other people exist and are deserving of our attention and respect. I'm not talking about our friends and family, though they certainly are deserving. In this case, I mean everyone else—the everyday people we see as we go about our business. Included are the ones we fail to hold the door open for, and the ones we forget to thank when they hold the door open for us. They are the ones we ignore while we check our latest email and the ones we don't acknowledge when they let us merge into their lane. It's not that these actions are rude, as much as they're not kind. The problem is, the more often we fail to be kind when we have the opportunity, the more common and accepted it will become.

You can help to change this. You can be kind to others. And, in the process, others will be encouraged to do so as well. Kindness is contagious. When someone has been treated nicely they're likely to pass it on to the next person they interact with. From there, who knows how far your one act of kindness can spread. What's great is it doesn't take much effort and it doesn't have to cost anything. All it takes to make someone else happy is a few nice words or a friendly gesture. That's it. A pleasant smile, a heartfelt compliment, or a hand when it's needed: *these are the actions that change lives.* They are small. They might appear unimportant. But these simple, seemingly meaningless acts are the keys to making the world a better place.

Life is not as easy as we'd like it to be. There are a lot of hardships to endure. We all carry a burden. Some are more difficult to deal with than others, but we all are struggling with something. It's important to remember that as bad as your burden may seem, there is always someone else who has it worse—someone who could use your support. Your traffic ticket is nothing compared to the person who just received that awful diagnosis from their doctor. So even though you may find yourself under a black cloud from time to time, do your best to step out from under it and make a positive impact in someone else's life.

Every day we have the opportunity to make others happy. Every passing moment is a chance to make a difference. You can ignore it or you can take advantage. No one is going to force you to do either, but if you choose to ignore the opportunity to be kind, not only will many miss out, but you will lose something as well. See, even though your motive should be to bring joy to someone else or ease their burden a bit, being kind to others will make *you* feel good, too. It's rewarding to know that another person is better off because of something you did or said. So do what you can to cheer them up. Lessen their load. Lift their spirits. Be the light that brightens their day.

#32

**Life changes on a dime.
Try to be two steps ahead.**

If there's one guarantee in life it's that you're going to be thrown curve balls. The unexpected has a way of happening just when you start to get comfortable with how things are. Sometimes it changes things just enough to push you off track, and other times it completely turns your life upside down. You usually don't know when or where these twists and turns will come from, so all you can do is think ahead. Be prepared for the unexpected. Try to anticipate what can go wrong, and have a plan for when it does. It's one thing to achieve the life you want, but in order to keep it you have to learn to adapt to uncertain conditions quickly.

You may know people who always seem to land on their feet. Even after the worst happens to them, once the dust settles, you notice they've ended up no worse than they were before. In fact, sometimes these people even manage to fall *upward*. Disaster strikes, and they turn out even *better* than they were before it happened. You probably wonder *how can this be?* It's most likely not a coincidence. Especially not when it's happened to them before. These are people who have prepared for the problems that may arise. Instead of resting on their laurels, they have continued to build their foundation, making it stronger and wider. They do everything they can to establish a safety net beneath them. This is not being cowardly or lacking confidence. This is being humble enough to know some things are out of their control, and smart enough to make sure they never fall too far.

As unpredictable as life is, and as important as it is to be prepared for the unexpected, there will be times when it never comes to pass. Sometimes the catastrophe is narrowly avoided, other times it never shows up at all. When this happens you might wonder whether the planning and preparation and caution was worth it. The answer is almost always *yes*. If the concern was reasonable and the potential for loss was great, then you can never go wrong taking precautions. It's better to have a Plan B and not need it. Not only are you better safe than sorry, but through preparation you line yourself up for other good fortune in the process. It's been said that luck is nothing more than what happens when preparation meets opportunity. If you don't put yourself in the right positions, good luck won't be able to find you. You can't win the lottery unless you buy a ticket.

Despite all your best efforts to prepare, misfortune may still strike. It might be in a way that you weren't expecting or at a moment that caught you off-guard. Whatever the case, don't let it get you down. Sometimes the things that seem like misfortunes are actually creating opportunities for something better to find you. Sometimes you have to lose everything before you can really gain anything. The truth is, no matter how much you prepare for disaster or how hard you try to catch problems before they occur, sometimes life just decides it's going to take you for a ride. When this happens, two steps ahead or not, all you can do is keep your hands inside the cart and see where it takes you.

#31
Technology is great, but remember, you can't hug through a text.

It's a great time to be alive. Technology is advancing rapidly, making our lives more convenient and enjoyable. There are gadgets for everything, and just about anyone you stop on the street will likely have a telephone, camera, calculator, flashlight and more in their pocket at any given time. And all built into one device. It's remarkable, when you think about it. It is also equally necessary. But not because we actually *need* these devices, as helpful as they are. Don't forget that humans existed for thousands and thousands of years just fine *without* these gadgets. No, we need them because we've forgotten (already) what it's like to sit idle. We are uncomfortable with silence. We don't know what to do with ourselves if we don't have some sort of screen to look at. At this point, what would anyone do without them?

I'll tell you what we'd do. We'd be forced to communicate...(gasp) verbally. We would have no choice but to speak to someone if we wanted them to know something. We would be more in tune with our surroundings and more attentive to our loved ones. We might not know what our friends did that day if we don't check our social networks, but so what? Unplugging ourselves from the rest of the cyber universe once in a while won't hurt. In fact, it might actually help. We might develop a new hobby, or meet a new friend. Maybe we notice the person who ends up being our spouse because we picked our heads up just long enough to see them walking by. Yes, all of these things can be done through technology too, but there is something about person to person contact that you just can't simulate electronically.

Throughout history, technological developments have propelled the human race ahead. We are so much better off because of these advancements. We are also worse off for them. Just as they've led to improvements in how we live, they've caused many problems as well. We shouldn't stop evolving technologies just because they've been abused or misused or have bad side effects. That would come at the expense of too much good. But they shouldn't be overused, either. The key to making technology work for us rather than becoming a slave to it is balance. Balance in our dependency on it. Balance in how and why we use it. Balance in the priority it takes in our lives. Don't neglect the important stuff. That new app can wait.

Many of us, me included, have gotten to the point where we don't even realize when we're head-down, nose-deep in our cell phones. It's a habit more than anything, and it goes back to what I said about not knowing what to do with idle time. It's actually good for our minds to not have anything occupying them once in a while. It's refreshing. It allows for an alternate perspective on life. Put your device down every so often, even if just for a moment. See the beauty around you. Watch your children play. Better yet, go play *with* them. Spend time with your friends and family. Don't live a virtual life at the expense of a real one, because remember, as great as technology is, you can't hug through a text.

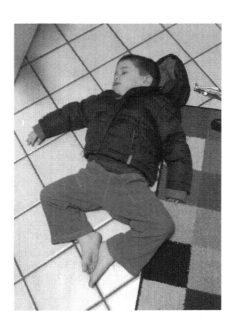

#30
If you're tired, sleep.

We all need rest. Our bodies need to be rejuvenated; our brains need to slow down. No matter how different two people are, they have at least one thing in common: sleep is necessary. Even though we know this, and can feel it, we still deprive ourselves of it. We go to bed too late and then have an early alarm the next morning. We need more sleep than we typically get, but we decide that we're doing it for good reasons. We're passing it up to work harder and achieve more, to separate ourselves from those mortals that surrender time to sleep. That might be what we tell ourselves, but the reality is we're actually hurting our ability to do those things. Sleep recharges us. Without it, we struggle to think clearly. We miss details. Without sleep, we are far from our best.

The secret to getting more done and doing it well isn't to work *longer*. The secret is to work *smarter*. There is much more time in a day than we actually use because we tend to procrastinate. We find distractions. The things we need to do are put off until we have no choice but to sacrifice sleep in order to complete them. Everyone does it, but the people that overcome the urge to put things off are the ones that notice when it's happening and quickly bring themselves back to the task at hand. Managing your time so that little is wasted will not only make you more productive, you'll also be less likely to cut into your sleep to complete your responsibilities. And, as a result, you'll be more focused and energetic throughout the day.

Still, no matter how prepared you are, or how well you manage your time, there will be days when you have no choice but to push through fatigue and just get things done. Things come up at the last minute, or take longer than you planned. Emergencies aren't concerned with your sleep quota. Although working while tired may be your only option, you will quickly realize why it's not ideal. The quality of your work suffers. The joy is often removed. Focus is fleeting. Any task is harder when you're tired. There is definitely a tipping point where it is no longer worthwhile to push ahead. Sometimes you have to work less now in order to get better results later. Sometimes rest is the best use of your time, no matter how limited that time may be.

We can go back and forth about when it's better to rest and when you should buckle down and do the work, but it's really pretty simple. Listen to your body. It will let you know when it needs a break. When it does, get some rest. This isn't permission to be lazy, this is a demand that you always give yourself the opportunity to be at the top of your game. You can't be your best without being rested. So learn to recognize when you need it, and if you're tired, sleep.

#29

There are days when even
the simplest task is difficult.

Things won't always be easy. You will have days when even the simplest task is difficult. There could be a number of reasons why, but sometimes things are just a little bit off, and we can't seem to get on track. Maybe you don't have much creative juice flowing, or your analytical thinking is broken down. It could be you're having a hard time concentrating on some tedious task you need to get done. Some days are just bad for meaningful productivity. It's a given that there will be times like this, and you can't always control when they happen, but you can control how you react to them. You can let it consume you, and get frustrated as you continue to bang your head against the wall trying to make it work. Or, you can acknowledge that something's not right and spend that time finding another way.

When you get tired of banging your head against the wall, you'll realize that the better choice is to find another way. That might mean going about it a little bit differently. Or, it might mean doing something else instead. In extreme cases, it might mean stepping away completely. Sometimes a break is the only cure. Of course, if you start to rely on this as your regular answer you will end up not accomplishing much of anything. There is a point where a long break turns into giving up. Something as simple and commonplace as a bad day should not be the reason you give up on anything. Taking a break is fine. But make it a short one. The longer you're away, the harder it is to get started again.

One of the best ways to stay productive—while avoiding the part that's got you held up—is to shift gears and try something else. If you're having trouble being creative, leave it alone and move on to something technical. If it's a technical issue that's got you bogged down, let your mind run free creatively. Not only will this keep you active and productive, the answer to your original problem might come to you once you've stepped away and put your mind on something else. Another reason this works is it keeps you from being idle. You are still making progress by letting your mind rest on one topic and attacking the one it is ready for. Whenever you have the choice, always follow inspiration. It is where your best and most honest work will come from.

If you try and try and try to find a way into the inspired part of your brain and still can't, you may want to consider calling it a day. When you force anything it usually ends up being a fraction of its potential. You become frustrated and since it's not good enough, you'll have to do it all again anyway. Step away and wait until you are having a better day. Don't be frustrated. Bad days happen to the best, most successful people. It's easy to get worked up and upset with yourself, but keep in mind that just like you're not always as good as your absolute best day, neither are you really as bad as your worst day. As long as the average of those days is something you are happy with, you have nothing to worry about.

#28
When you see someone who ignores it, you'll realize how important hygiene is.

Personal hygiene is important for all the obvious reasons. Nobody wants to have bad breath breathed on them. Long, unkempt fingernails collect all sorts of dirt and grime. Teeth that aren't brushed will get really, really ugly before they finally fall out. The list goes on and on. Maintaining your hygiene is just another part of presenting the best version of yourself. It's also one of those things that are rarely noticed unless they are ignored. In other words, it's a thankless chore, a pesky necessity that is expected but likely won't earn you a "thatta boy" or a "nice work." Of course, that's not why you cut your nails. You don't do it to receive compliments. You do it to maintain your health and to keep a clean appearance. Mostly, you do it because the alternative is less than ideal.

When stress begins to pile up, one of the first things we tend to do is spend less time on ourselves. It's easy to neglect those little things when much larger, more pressing issues are bearing down on you, but as normal and common as that is, it only serves to make things worse. Those are the times when you need to take *even greater* care of yourself. It may not seem like much, but your physical health plays a very big role in your ability to handle stress. And one of the simplest ways to control your health is through good hygiene habits. Brushing your teeth may not take the pressure off you at work, but it sure won't help things in the office if you develop a cavity and need to miss a day to get it pulled. Those preventative measures are the small necessities that gain only a little on the surface, but will cost you a lot if ignored.

In any task, project or competition the key to whether they're successful or not often boils down to the little things. With regard to taking care of yourself, personal hygiene is "the little things." The tiny details that seem like they can be skipped without much consequence are actually the most crucial. They represent an attention to detail that can—and will—carry over to the rest of your life. When you commit to respecting the small details in anything you do, the big things will fall into place more easily. It's about developing good habits that will stay with you for a long time. As soon as you give yourself a little room to cheat or make exceptions, it becomes that much easier for those habits to die off. Self-discipline is doing things you might not want to do now, because you know you'll be glad you did later.

See, there is much more to be gained from having good hygiene than pearly whites and smelling nicely. Make a commitment to address the little things in your life and your work. Take your health seriously. Develop good habits so those details become second nature. Pay attention to the role each detail plays. And definitely don't ignore them. It won't take long for you to see how important they really are.

#27

You've already put your mother through enough. Go easy on her.

Childbirth is traumatic for everyone involved. When you were born, I was the least imposed upon, and it still took quite a toll on me. I can't imagine what it was like for you or your mother. As little more than a witness, I can tell you I experienced the full gamut of emotions that day. I was excited. I was scared. I was nervous, anxious, ready, unprepared, happy and hungry. I was a little angry too, but that's because I get that way when I'm hungry. Still, I felt all of these things *before* we even really got started helping you into the world. Once that whole process began, my mind was completely blown. Childbirth is the most remarkable and amazing thing I've ever seen. It gave me an entirely new level of respect for women. I am not sure I could have gone through what the mother has to. But your mom can. She did. And she did it for you.

The fact that she happily put her body through all the changes that it went through, with the understanding that it probably would never be the same again as a result, is reason enough to earn your respect. So give it to her. She is your mom—your only one—and she loved you before she ever met you. She made you her first priority long before she ever saw your face, let alone held you in her arms. She has, and will continue to, sacrifice her wants and needs to make sure yours are taken care of. And she would still do all of those things, even if you never showed her how grateful you are—because that's what moms do. Knowing all of this, how can you have anything but love and respect for her? How can you not be thankful that you have someone in your corner who would do anything for you?

It's natural that she'll have your back and support you. She'll always do what she can to make sure you're happy. She'll continue making sacrifices for you, many of which you won't even know about. But that's not to say she's going to be perfect all the time. Even though her intentions will always be good, and her actions will always be based on what she thinks is best for you, she will make mistakes. She will do things that upset you. Love her anyway. Sometimes you will think she's being unfair. Respect her anyway. No matter how much you disagree with her decisions, she's still your mother. Together, she and I are doing the best we can, and most of the time, we're learning as we go.

When you feel the urge to give her a hard time because she exposes herself as the imperfect parent that she is—that *all* parents are—remember all the things she's already done for you. Remind yourself of the sacrifices she made before she even knew you. Understand that she is not out to get you, and that everything she does, and has *ever* done, is directly inspired by one thing: love. Show her some of that love in return. Give her a break once in a while. Go easy on her. You've already put her through enough.

#26

You can't always do it by yourself.
It's okay to ask for help.

We all have limitations. We all have weaknesses. Everyone needs help from time to time. No matter how good you are, or how much success you've achieved, there will be things you struggle with. The real weakness doesn't lie in not being able to do something, it lies in failing to acknowledge that you may need some help. It's great to have confidence in your ability to do anything you set out to do, but don't fool yourself into thinking it's always going to come naturally and easily. Standing in your way could be a lack of time or experience or talent, but regardless of the cause, there is no shame in asking for a hand. Nobody expects you to immediately be good at *everything*, so you shouldn't expect it of yourself, either. Take on challenges. Give new things a try. But if you get stuck, it's okay to find someone that can help you.

When you ask for help you increase the chances you'll get it done, for sure. But you also benefit in other ways. You learn new ideas and techniques that you might not have been exposed to otherwise. You gain confidence in yourself, because now that you've seen what it takes, you're more likely to be able to do it next time. Or, you might realize that you had no business trying it on your own in the first place, and that it's best outsourced from now on— a discovery that could save you frustrations down the road. Either way, accepting help is not an admission of incompetence. It's not a reflection of your worth. It's proof that you understand your strengths and recognize your weaknesses. It allows you to get past the parts you're not as good at and focus on the ones you are. And, it will save you the most finite resource of all: time.

There is only so much time available to us. Even the things you are capable of doing might not be the best use of your time. Sometimes asking for help is a way of freeing you up to do what you do best. Most people have a hard time delegating responsibility because it's human nature to believe others won't do things as well as you. And that may be true—especially when you're measuring by your own standards—but if someone else can take a task off of your plate, and do it to a level that is satisfactory, let them do it. When you put too much on your own shoulders, at best you sacrifice quality, and at worst you run the risk of burning yourself out. Neither leads to good outcomes.

You may worry what others will think if you ask them or anyone else for help. Maybe they'll judge you as someone who lacks ability or is not to be taken seriously. Maybe they'll think you're lazy. If they do, that's their problem. Asking for help doesn't make you less of a man—it makes you a smart man. When you acknowledge that you need a hand, you are putting yourself in a better position to succeed. A touch of humility never hurt anyone. In fact, it can serve you well. Accept the fact that you don't know everything, and that there might be someone out there who can teach you a thing or two. Don't let your pride stand in the way of accomplishing more. You can't always do it by yourself. Sometimes, it's okay to ask for help.

#25

People have a 5-second rule, too.
Pick yourself up quickly.

There is a 5-second rule that applies to people, though it doesn't involve eating or falling on the floor—at least not literally. The 5-second rule that applies to us is our ability to "get up" when we "fall" into hard times. When things aren't going our way, or we've failed at something, how quickly can we pick ourselves back up and move on? How enthusiastically do we regroup and give it another try? The quicker we do, the less likely we are to be contaminated by self-doubt, and the smaller the opportunity for despair. Much is often made of the importance of not giving up, but trying again is *not* the only answer. You need to try again *soon*. You can't give hopelessness and fear enough time to get a hold of you, because their grip is strong, and once they do, it's hard to get them to let go.

The important thing to remember when you do give it another try is that just doing the same thing is not the answer. Falling short usually happens because there was some flaw in your plan or some error in the execution. You can't expect to do it the same way again and have a different result. That's why regrouping is key. Evaluate and consider other options before you fire away again. Going back to the drawing board is still a form of picking yourself up. You haven't given up; you're not sulking in your own self-pity. You're back at it, but instead of doing something that's failed before, you're devising a better, more informed strategy—one that will be less likely to cause you to fall down again.

The nature of the world is that you're likely to take a lot of punches before you finally land one of your own. If you stay down the first time you're punched, no one will hear much about you again. But if you get back up, taking as many punches as are necessary until you finally get one in yourself, you send a message to anyone you meet that you are resilient, that you are determined, and that you won't go away easily. Not only does each punch bring you one step closer, they help to show you the way, too. Every stumble is like a pin on a map marking where you've been, and giving you a nudge to the left or to the right, helping you to find your destination.

In order for any of this to work, you have to accept the fact that you are going to fall down at one time or another. If you haven't fallen, that's a clue that you aren't taking enough risk—that you aren't testing yourself. It might be more comfortable to play it safe—and not stick your neck out—but one day you'll regret the things you didn't do, the chances you didn't take, and the dreams you didn't chase. You might come up short. It's possible you will fail. But that's okay. Those aren't outcomes, they are stepping stones. They're just part of the process, provided you don't quit. And thankfully, you don't have to. There's a 5-second rule that applies to us, and using it allows us to rise above failure, to learn from our mistakes and come back stronger. All we have to do is pick ourselves back up.

#24

Thinking is exercise for your mind.
Make it a habit.

We know how important it is to exercise our body and keep it in good shape. We obsess over our weight and our appearance, setting goals and then checking the scale (and the mirror) to gauge our progress. It's good to take care of our bodies, but sometimes we become so concerned with fitting into our pants that we forget to put the same attention toward improving our minds as well. Just like our bodies, our brains need exercise. They need to be challenged and tested. If we don't use them regularly, they grow weak. But if we do set aside time, every day, to give them the exercise they need, there's no limit to how strong they can become.

Our days are very full. We end up with so much on our minds that we don't know how to make room for them to relax. They become clouded with garbage and meaningless details—the mental equivalent of what fast food does to our bodies. Watch out for this, and when it starts to become too much, consider putting your brain on a diet. Filter out the things that make it bloated and over-worked. Avoid exposing it to information you simply don't need. Allowing too much debris in there will leave it running slower and less effectively. Instead, clear out space by meditating or getting lost in thought. It's okay to let your mind wander. Let it ponder big problems and tiny dilemmas. Free it up to go where it wants. Many answers are discovered that way.

Just like with your body, for it to really benefit, you can't only exercise your mind once in a while. It's got to be done regularly—every day, if possible—because the effects compound themselves. You get better at it, and are more productive each time. As you get older, it will naturally start to slip (metabolism of the mind), making it even more important to give it the attention it needs. The more time you spend exercising your mind, the greater its capabilities become. It will stay sharper longer—both throughout the day, and your lifetime. Habits you form now will certainly pay off later, so find things you enjoy that make you think critically and strategical-ly. Take up hobbies that encourage an active mind. They will bene-fit you for the rest of your life.

When was the last time you completely disconnected from everything else and just *thought?* It could be about anything—deep topics without absolute answers, or simple things you normally overlook. When was the last time you pushed your brain to work a little harder? The last time you challenged it to expand its under-standing or beliefs? There are so many ways we can grow and im-prove ourselves, and each of them plays a role in our overall devel-opment, but none is more important or beneficial than regularly exercising our brains. That's what thinking does for us. I encourage you to make it a habit.

#23

They're called con • SUCK • uences for a reason.
Stay out of trouble.

One of the first things we learn is that there are consequences for our actions. If you touch the hot stove, you are going to get burned. If you talk back to your parents, you are going to get grounded. If you do the wrong thing, you are going to be punished. It's not pleasant, but it's a necessary way of life. Repercussions help to keep the world in order. Without them, everyone would run around doing whatever they wanted and there would be chaos. Knowing that our actions have consequences encourages us to make good decisions. We are less likely to do wrong because the penalty is not worth it. Even when morals and ethics aren't good enough reasons to do the right thing, the threat of consequences helps to keep us on track.

Sometimes it's tempting to do or say things that we know will get us into trouble. No matter how tempted you may be, keep in mind that it's almost never worth it. We often let emotions get the best of us in these situations, and not long afterward we realize how foolish or embarrassing our behavior was. Unfortunately, by then it's usually too late to take back, and an apology only goes so far. Even if you are forgiven, you'll still have to deal with any consequences that came from your actions. And, sometimes, those consequences extend even further than you realize. You never know who might be watching you. Bad decisions you make now have a habit of popping up later, often at the worst possible times and in the most damaging ways.

So many of our decisions are based on instant gratification, without any long-term or big-picture thinking. We see something we want and we take it. It might be satisfying at that moment, but this kind of behavior is very dangerous. It can lead down some troublesome roads. Avoid making rash decisions. Think things through and consider the possible outcomes of your choices. The right decision isn't always cut-and-dry, and there are likely to be gray areas or uncertainties. Sometimes, even when all the information is available to you, there's no way to know which will turn out to be the best decision. In those cases, the best advice is to listen to your gut. When in doubt, follow its guidance, even if it goes against what you want right now. Our instincts will often nudge us one way or the other, and more often than not, they're right.

Knowing that a wrong decision could cause you problems can be intimidating at times. But, you still have to live your life. Don't let the threat of bad consequences paralyze you with fear. Just be aware of their existence and their power. Respect their ability to interrupt your progress and set you back. And avoid them as well as you can. Consequences are a necessary part of life, but they shouldn't control you. They are there to encourage you to do the right thing and to remind you when you don't. Remember, they're called con•SUCK•uences for a reason. Most of the time, they aren't much fun. Do your best to stay out of trouble.

#22
I'm glad you can hear, but it's important you listen.

There is a huge difference between hearing and listening. The ability to hear is natural, and one that most of us are born with. It just happens, whether you are aware or not. I'm happy that you can hear; I'm thankful that you were born healthy. However, being able to hear isn't enough. It's important that you learn how to listen. Listening is something that you consciously choose to do. It requires focus and concentration. It demands your attention, and as a result, you are provided with information. Listening offers you an opportunity to learn—about a subject, about the speaker, and sometimes, about yourself. Hearing is a passive ability. You just do it. But listening is an active *skill*. It's something you have to constantly work on to improve. You can always become a better listener.

When you listen actively, you are more likely to remember what you are hearing. Small details are absorbed more accurately. For example, I have a bad habit of not actively listening when someone tells me their name when I meet them for the first time. I'm not sure why, but it's a *very* bad habit. If I don't make it a point to listen, I'm less likely to remember their name even just a couple minutes later. Now, imagine doing this when you are listening to a teacher, or your boss, or anyone else who may have a lot of information for you. You might *hear* them, but if you're not *listening* you won't remember a thing they said. Active listening is the best way to retain that information and be able to recall it when needed. Improving your listening skills takes practice, and a concentrated effort, but the benefits are worth it.

Aside from retaining information—ranging from big ideas to tiny details—another benefit of careful listening is the opportunity to "hear" things that aren't being said. Sometimes people tell us things by hinting at them. They might insinuate an idea or belief—perhaps without even realizing it—and if you are paying attention, you can make sense of those clues. It can give you a critical advantage in a negotiation or help you discover what's really upsetting a family member. Listening involves more than just words. It uses body language, tone and inflection to create a complete image. It helps us to *truly* understand. In many ways, our ability to listen is more important than our ability to talk. When you talk, you only say things *you* already know, but when you listen, you learn things *others* know.

Listening does a lot for you. It helps you learn. It helps you understand. It also does something for the person you're listening to. It makes them feel important. It makes them feel loved and respected. It makes them feel like someone cares about their concerns, knowledge or opinions. When you listen to someone—I mean *really* listen, as if what they have to say is the most important thing in the world—you endear yourself to them. They will remember their "conversation" with you, even if you barely speak. You will leave an impression. And, in the process, you may learn a thing or two.

#21

Anyone who tells you "That's impossible!" obviously doesn't know you well enough.

You can do anything you want to do. People may try to tell you otherwise, but those people obviously don't know the kind of person you are. They don't know about your self-confidence, or your ability to turn dreams into reality. They don't know that you are not going to give in without trying, or that you are not going to take someone else's word for it. And they certainly don't know that you are not going to let other people dictate what you are or aren't capable of doing. If they did, they wouldn't bother doubting you. They'd save their breath instead. The only limits to your potential are the ones you place on yourself. No matter what others think or say or do to discourage you, they cannot hold you back unless you allow it. Let them talk. Let them laugh at you, if it makes them feel better. Then go out and show them how wrong they were.

Think about some of the most amazing accomplishments people have made. Building an airplane. Walking on the moon. Talking over the telephone. Now imagine if the Wright brothers or Neil Armstrong or Alexander Graham Bell listened to the naysayers and gave up. Think about where we'd be now as a result. Sure, someone else may have come along and done it anyway, but that's the point—*someone else* would be the one to do it. If *you* are going to be the one to see your dreams come true, and achieve the goals and aspirations you have for yourself, you can't listen when people doubt them. Remain convinced that it *can* be done, and that *you* can be the one who does it. It takes a brave person to see possibility in the impossible and an even braver one to chase it. But, eventually, someone will have the courage to do it. Why not let it be you?

When someone tries to discourage you from chasing "impossibility", take a minute to consider their motive. Are they a friend? A family member? How much do you value their opinion? Are they a known pessimist? Is this someone you *need* to associate with? If you don't need them, and they do you more harm than good, disassociate yourself. Spend less (or zero) time around them and remove their ability to fill your head with doubt. Even if the doubter is someone you want to remain friends with—or maybe a family member that you can't cut out of your life completely—don't talk to them about the "impossible" task any more than you have to. Keep your relationship with them separate from your challenging goal. Don't give them a chance to second-guess your abilities.

If you've taken it upon yourself to aim for something so challenging that others will doubt whether you can do it, you probably won't need much outside motivation to get it done. You probably already have the internal drive that's necessary, but even the most confident people have moments of doubt. Even the most deter-mined have times where they wonder if they've bitten off more than they can chew. When you need a little extra push—a little bit more motivation to accomplish the impossible—think of those that questioned you. Remember how they told you it couldn't be done, and that you are foolish for trying. Use their doubt as fuel to inspire you. Show them what you're really like, because anyone who tells you "That's impossible!" obviously doesn't know you well enough.

#20

There's a fine line between being the life of the party and partying your life away.

The class clown gets laughs. The party animal has a lot of friends. It can seem like a good thing when you're the center of attention for acting wild and carefree. People love you; they want to be around you. But when it goes too far, or carries on too long, this behavior can be very, very harmful. What starts off as a joke in class might turn into disrespecting a teacher. Going out too much could turn into alcoholism or experimenting with drugs. One moment you're feeling great and enjoying life, and the next minute you're trying to repair an image or correct a mistake that's difficult to take back. Yes, they are extreme examples of what could happen, but the line that separates each extreme is narrow and it can be crossed quickly and without much warning.

When you feel like you have everything under control it's easy to scoff at this idea, but if you live too close to this line for too long, you will eventually cross it. And the more time you spend on the wrong side, the harder it is to cross back. The barrier between appropriate and overboard will get cloudier and cloudier until you can no longer recognize it. Throughout it all you may still have some "supporters"—those who have either already lost their own way or care so little about you that they have no problem watching you crash and burn. To be clear: they are *not* your friends. Real friends wouldn't encourage that behavior. Not only would they not encourage it, they would drag you away by your ears before watching you get yourself in that kind of trouble.

Another thing to remember about going too far and having too much fun: those thrills are fleeting. The damage will catch up to you eventually. It's like a delayed hangover. You feel no effects while you're doing it. Actually, you are probably really, really enjoying yourself, oblivious to the damage you're doing and the pain you're causing. But suddenly, one day—without much warning at all—you wake up and you've lost something. In some cases, you could wake up to realize you've lost *everything*. All the "friends" are long gone. Your family is tired. Your boss is fed up. The cheers and laughs and pats on the back are echoes in your memory. That is no way to live. It's tempting on the surface, sure, but it doesn't last. It's really not all that great, either. It's artificial happiness, and it carries side effects that are not worth it.

I'm not telling you not to go out and have a good time. It's okay to be the center of attention and entertain others, but like anything else in life, it's *got* to be done in moderation. Stay away from drugs. Use alcohol legally and responsibly. Most of all, don't allow yourself to depend on these things to have fun. The true life of the party is someone who can find fun in any situation and without any stimuli. If this is you, great. And if that's not you, fine, but don't try to become that person by partying hard and recklessly. There is a fine line between being the life of the party and partying your life away. Please, please, *please* walk it carefully.

#19

Celebrate your successes.
It's ok to be proud of your achievements.

Many of us have a hard time recognizing and celebrating our own successes. We might be embarrassed. Or we fail to realize their importance. Or we think others will consider us arrogant, conceited or self-absorbed. Those reasons are understandable, but they shouldn't discourage you from letting people know about the great things you've done. If you've done something awesome, tell someone. Tell a lot of people. Celebrate it. Be proud of your accomplishments. Anyone that has worked hard to achieve something themselves will understand your excitement. It probably wasn't easy. It's likely that time and effort and frustration were all part of the process, and if you've still succeeded, it's something to celebrate. So do it. And don't feel bad about it. Take credit where credit is due.

At the same time, don't ever take *all* the credit. No matter how much you had to do with the success, someone *must* have helped you along the way. Even if every single idea was yours and each step of the project came from your efforts, there had to be *someone* who inspired you. Or someone who relieved you of other responsibilities so you could get it done. Always remember that you never truly do anything on your own. And even if you think you did, find someone else to share the praise with. Acknowledge *everyone* that played a part in your success—no matter how small their role may have been. Thank them for their help and make the achievement theirs as much as yours. It's the right thing to do, and it will make it even easier for others to be happy for you. Not only that, but they will be eager to help you again in the future, knowing that you appreciate and value what they do.

When you do sing your own praises (or those of your group) you might encounter people who respond with criticism or cynicism. They might try to belittle your achievement or one-up you. Pay no attention. If you are proud of yourself, don't let the opinions of critics bring you down. Maybe they're jealous. Maybe they're angry. Maybe they honestly think you did a lousy job and don't deserve the attention you're getting. That's not your problem. If you've accomplished a goal, and you're happy that you did, be proud. You can't control the behaviors of other people, and the only way their opinions affect you is if you decide to let them. As long as you are content with what you've done, forget about what anyone else thinks. Turn your focus to your next great accomplishment.

As important as it is to celebrate when you've done well, one of the biggest mistakes you can make is to celebrate prematurely.

You've seen the team that begins crowning themselves victors only to watch their opponents take the win from them at the last minute. Don't take your foot off the pedal until the job is 100% completed. See it through to the end. Then, when it's all done, when you've reached that big goal, you can look back and be proud of what you accomplished. And even if others aren't as excited for you, you'll know what it took. The hard work—the blood, the sweat, and the tears—will have finally paid off. You deserve to be happy. You are allowed to be excited. It's okay to be proud.

#18

Toot your own horn in moderation.
Nobody likes a braggart.

Celebrating when you do well is a good thing. Telling others about your accomplishment is fine, too. But be careful how far you take it. Beware of sounding cocky or arrogant. Be sure not to rub your success in the faces of others who haven't been as fortunate. Your grandpa always told me, *"When you win say little, when you lose say less."* It's fine to be proud of the things you've done—and to some degree your future opportunities will come from your ability to sell previous accomplishments—but there's something to be said for being humble, too. It takes a special person to stay the same despite all the accolades, fame and fortune. You want to be someone who can do all those awesome things without letting it go to their head, someone who doesn't let it change who they are.

If you position yourself as a person who achieves much but doesn't over-sing his own praises, not only will you gain many supporters, you may also see them become more eager to do the singing for you. They will be happy to tell others about you because they will admire you for your talents, and also because of your humility. For that to happen, you must learn how to promote your abilities without overdoing it. You have to display confidence in yourself without letting it turn into cockiness. You can become someone that others will root for by staying grounded in your success and showing how grateful you are for it. Give thanks for the help you've received from others, and acknowledge how fortunate you have been. You can be proud and humble at the same time.

No matter how much success you may have, people don't want to be around someone who is constantly reminding them of it. Not only do they not want to hear about it all the time, they may end up secretly hoping you'll stumble, just to bring you down to earth a little bit. In some cases—when the arrogance has gone too far—you could find them openly rooting against you. It takes quite a bit to get people to this point, but the last thing you want is for your talents and accomplishments to be overshadowed by a repulsive personality. Instead of using your platform to crow, use it to grow. Take advantage of the attention your success gets by building alliances, by networking, and by helping others to reach their own goals. You are not the only person who has ever found success, nor will you be the last. So don't act like it.

There *is* a time and place for celebrating your accomplishments, and by no means do I think you should ignore or minimize them. Just be aware that you can celebrate too often or too proudly. Find the careful balance between promoting your achievements and boasting. Whenever possible let your work, and those that admire it, speak for you. Be proud of what you've done, but remember what it took to get there. Stay humble, and most importantly, don't take anything for granted, because it can all be taken from you in a moment.

#17

**People may try to feast on
your generosity and compassion.
Don't let them change who you are.**

I hope you'll grow up to be a kind, compassionate person—someone who is aware of the needs of others and does what he can to help. I hope that you'll always try to see the good in a person, even when they've done their best to bury it deep beneath anger and hatred and selfishness. I want you to do your best to avoid judging someone based on the tiny bit you may know about them, because what you see may just be the tip of the iceberg. Under the water could lie a beautiful person who has been beaten down by life, and you may be the boost they need to pick themselves back up again. I encourage you to see someone you love in the homeless person begging for food. How would you want *your* loved one treated?

Unfortunately, wherever there is generosity and selflessness, there are people looking to take advantage. Like sharks, they circle around waiting for their chance to feast on that kindness. They live very much in the moment, and when they see an opportunity, they take it. Maybe it's the panhandler who isn't really as bad off as they make themselves out to be. Maybe it's the person who is accepting donations for an illness that doesn't exist. Maybe it's the fundraiser that is playing "two for me, one for you" when donations come in for someone who really needs it. As deplorable as these actions are, don't let them affect your compassion towards those who need your help. For every one scam artist, there are dozens of real people in need.

Along the way, there's a good chance you might help someone who turns out to be dishonest, or maybe you suspect they are without knowing for sure. In the grand scheme of things, it doesn't matter. What matters is that you tried to help someone else. You did what you could do to make their life easier. There *is* room for intrinsic reward when you take up charitable causes or drop some change in a cup on the sidewalk. If the person you helped misuses the money, so be it. There's not much you can do about that. But you can (and should) be happy knowing you made an effort to help someone less fortunate than you. You *should* feel good about what you did. And you *should* continue to do it, whenever you are able, because being kind to just one deserving person more than makes up for all the frauds.

Nobody wants to be taken advantage of, and I would hate to see someone exploit your big heart. But I would be even more disappointed to see you grow coldhearted instead. To watch you lose faith in humanity would be a shame. Thankfully, there's a lot of goodness in the world. There are *many* ordinary people doing *many* great things every day. Align yourself with these people. Follow their example. Take up the challenge to leave this world a better place than you found it. That kind of impact takes dedication and commitment. It takes a person who is willing to risk being exploited in order to help someone else. It takes someone who is determined to show generosity and compassion, and who refuses to let the sharks change who they are.

#16

Think things through before acting,
and you'll have less to apologize for.

Saying "I'm sorry" is difficult. Apologizing means owning up to a mistake you've made. It means showing weakness as you acknowledge that you've come up short or done others wrong. Sometimes it opens you up to criticism or backlash. It can be a hit on your ego, and it can validate the efforts or opinions of your biggest rival. None of that is fun or pleasant. Swallowing your pride might be uncomfortable—especially when emotions are still high—but sometimes it's the right thing to do. It's a gesture that goes a long way toward preserving or mending relationships. Even the most confrontational person will have a hard time debating with you when all you have to offer them is an apology. Apologizing helps you to remove anger or guilt that you might be carrying. It frees you up to live life without the burden that ongoing conflicts create. It allows you to have peace of mind.

Even though an apology goes a long way toward fixing a situation, sometimes saying "I'm sorry" isn't enough. If you intentionally hurt someone and then try to apologize, don't be surprised if they don't forgive you right away. Having a willingness to apologize does not give you a free pass to be rude or hateful. It's not permission to mistreat others, and you shouldn't treat it as such. An apology might help to ease the pain, but it doesn't automatically make people forget. It doesn't wipe the slate completely clean. There are almost always scars left behind which may take years to go away— if they ever do. When you tell someone you're sorry for pain you've caused, it's a step in the right direction, but it is rarely ever a fix-all.

There is a way that you can limit how often you are faced with having to apologize. It involves some self-control and forethought. If you take a moment before you do something, and think about the potential consequences, you may avoid having to apologize later. Consider how your actions might affect another person, or how badly your words might sting them, and if it feels like that behavior could cause trouble, maybe you should try another way instead. The heat of the moment usually involves impulse and emotion, and they are a very dangerous combination. If you act solely on their behalf, you will find yourself needing to apologize often. But if you take a deep breath first, and consider the effects your actions will have, potential problems can, and will, be avoided.

Honest mistakes are much more acceptable than carelessness. If your intentions are in the right place and things just don't go as planned, that is unfortunate but it can often be corrected. Fractured relationships are more likely to be repaired when the cause is a mistake. But a complete disregard for other people and their feelings is inexcusable. It's selfish to act without consideration for others, and it's hard to expect them to readily forgive you afterward. Make every effort you can to get things right the first time. Don't put yourself in the position of always having to explain your behavior. Say you're sorry when you should, but if you think things through before acting, you'll have less to apologize for.

#15

Being the big brother is a big responsibility, probably the biggest.

As the oldest sibling, you have a responsibility to set a good example for the others. It's your job to show them how they should behave. You are under more scrutiny because, as they say, impressionable minds are always watching. Anything you do, they are likely to do as well. People are counting on you to lead by example. I know it's not something you asked for, but it happened anyway. Being the big brother makes you a role model by default. In many ways it makes you both the trailblazer and the scapegoat. Your siblings will undoubtedly benefit from the roads you pave for them, and you will probably face some hard times as well. It's a big responsibility, but as difficult as it can be, it's worth it.

Before you curse your birthright, keep in mind that this role is not limited only to the big brother. Anyone can be a role model. In fact, in a way, *everyone is* a role model. We all have an opportunity to set an example, and every day our actions do just that. We can inspire or we can discourage, simply by the decisions we make. The more successful you become, the more people your decisions will affect, but whether it's large scale or just your younger siblings, *somebody* is being influenced by what you do. Protect them from harm, but don't shelter them from the ways of the world. Show them how to find their own way, and when you get lost, call on your own role model to help you find the way again.

Being someone that others look up to can give your ego a nice boost. It's a good feeling to know that you are admired. Of course, it comes with expectations as well. When someone admires you they will tend to follow your example. The things you say and do—*everything* you say and do—will be observed, dissected and most likely mimicked. You will be expected to make good decisions. Those who admire you will *expect* you to do the right thing all the time. Just the fact that I'm writing these lessons will raise expectations that you always follow them and never make mistakes. That's okay, but always remember that, at one time or another, *everyone* makes mistakes. You will too. Own up to them. Correct them. Let your response be an example that others can follow when *they* mess up.

Life is not fair. Being born into a position of leadership may be a perfect example of exactly how unfair it can be. The pressure is high, the responsibility is overwhelming, the expectations are unrealistic, but the potential reward is *great*. When you have someone else looking up to you, you can easily feel how much your life matters. You are being counted on to lead the way, to show them how it's done and to give them hope that they can do it too. Your successes become theirs, and one day, theirs will be yours as well.

Your potential impact on the world has been multiplied, and its effects can be exponentially good or bad. It's up to you. In your lifetime, you will have many big responsibilities. Being the big brother just might be the biggest.

#14
We all have a story to tell.
Tell yours with passion.

You are here for a reason. You have a purpose to fulfill during your lifetime. It may not be clear right now what that purpose is or how you are going to accomplish it, but it's there. And it's your job to find it. Some people know right away what they are here to do, and they don't waste a moment working toward it. Others spend most of their lives trying to discover their purpose only to realize they've been living it all along. There are still others who never feed the desire to discover their purpose. They might be unmotivated or afraid or confused but, whatever the cause, they decide to let life go as it may, without ever searching for their true calling. And, as a result, they never find it.

Everyone is entitled to live the way they choose, but failing to find your purpose will likely leave you unfulfilled. There will always be something missing. Even if you lead a long and happy life, that one un-scratchable itch will remain. It sits there—sometimes quietly, other times painfully loud—eating away at you until you notice it. And it won't go away until you scratch. So scratch it. Allow yourself to become the person you are here to be. Live your life with purpose. To do otherwise will rob the world of what you have to offer and, more tragically, it will rob you of realizing your potential. We were never intended to go through the motions. You were not born to walk mindlessly through life. You are here because, like everyone else, there is a greater purpose to your existence. We all have a story to tell. Tell yours with passion.

In order to tell your story with passion, you have to block out all the noise and listen to your heart. To find your purpose you must acknowledge what fuels your ambition. What makes you feel alive and connected to the world? You'll know when you find it because you won't be able to imagine yourself doing anything else. What is considered "work" to others will feel like play to you. It will be something you can't see yourself tiring from. It will bring out the best in you, and it will be an example for anyone you meet. Your passion will inspire them to tell their stories and to live their lives in a way that fulfills them. In many ways, fulfilling your purpose will show you the difference between "living" and simply "being alive."

Once you've discovered the story you are supposed to tell, telling it will come so naturally that you will wonder why you took so long to get started. You might even find yourself frustrated at the time "wasted" before you found your calling. That's a normal reaction, but don't overlook the road you had to travel to get there. Sometimes there is only one path, and it might be full of bends and turns and maybe even a few dead ends. Sometimes it takes a number of experiences before you're ready to live your purpose. Sometimes you have to push through uncertainty and setbacks long enough to give your purpose a chance to find *you*. But if you are aware that there's a great story you were sent here to tell, and if you are committed to telling it with passion—whatever "it" may be— then when the day comes for you to start sharing it, you will be ready.

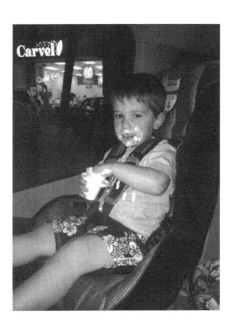

#13

Streamline your life.
Cut out the middleman. Simplify.

We're busy. Life is complex. There are always places to be and things to do, and it seems impossible to keep up. So we devise systems and tools, and rely on them to tell us where to be and what to do and how it should be done. We come up with fancy ways to do things and complicated methods for tracking them. Sometimes all these things work. And sometimes they don't. But even if they do, ask yourself if they're *necessary*. Consider the possibility that they are just one more thing for you to manage—one more thing to think about—and that maybe they aren't carrying their own weight. Are these tools adding to the clutter in your head and in your life? Are they helping you more than they're hurting you? Because if they aren't making things easier, if they're not worth the time, cut them.

Simplicity is a lost art. We've begun to think that bigger is better. We always want more and we have forgotten how to function without having something to preoccupy us. It's okay to do things the old-fashioned way. It's okay to remove the bells and whistles that do little more than bog us down and distract. You may miss the flash at first, but eventually you'll understand that you are actually *more* efficient without it. You'll appreciate that a clear mind is much more valuable to you than an extra feature or a new system. You'll come to realize that simpler is almost always better. The less there is to something, the less that can go wrong. And the less that goes wrong, the more time you have to focus on what's important.

As ideal as it is to try to streamline your life, not everything is that simple. Sometimes the systems *are* what's best for what we're trying to do. Sometimes the middleman *is* necessary—beneficial, even. Sometimes we have no choice but to embrace complexity, because the things we're attempting to make sense of are so complex themselves. This just makes it that much more important to simplify the things you can. Life is complicated enough on its own without us trying to make it more difficult. When you encounter a task, or an activity, or a moment that is just fine in its natural form, *enjoy it.* Don't ask why it's so simple. Don't complicate things. Don't add steps for the sake of adding steps. Just appreciate the "quiet."

Even when you are forced to live in a complex world, the "quiet" still exists. There is always an opportunity to find and enjoy simplicity. You might have to create it yourself. You might have to force yourself to take the time to "see" it, but when you do, you'll realize how refreshing simplicity can be. You'll also realize that the world doesn't stop when you unplug yourself. We don't *have* to move a mile a minute. We don't *need* to be hustling onward and upward every minute of every day. It's okay to take a break. Sometimes it's okay to just *be*. When you allow yourself the freedom to simply exist, you'll understand the value in existing simply.

#12

Work while others rest;
dream while others sleep.

So, if we've all got talents and we're all built for success, what separates those who achieve from those that don't? It's not ability. Ability is abundant. It's not desire. People with desire are a dime a dozen. The separation of someone who *has* potential from someone who *realizes* their potential comes from the willingness to *do*. You can't accomplish anything worthwhile, or become the person you want to become, unless you take action. You have to put those talents to work on a regular basis. And you have to be willing to do what others aren't. Make the sacrifices that are necessary to reach the top. Be sure they align with your priorities and values, then make them without a second thought. Those sacrifices will pay off

---

and when they do, you'll be among the few who benefit. The extra mile is never crowded, despite the fact that that's where most of the rewards lie.

Even though there are more than enough to go around, the spoils tend to go to the person that works the hardest. Life is competitive. And if your competition is working harder than you, or sacrificing things you aren't willing to sacrifice, they will have the edge when you meet. The difference between getting what you want and coming up short is usually microscopic. It's one little thing here, or one tiny detail there. It's the commitment to forfeit a night out with friends because you want to be well-rested for your performance the next morning. It means putting down the video games or turning off the computer to spend that extra hour practicing. It is making sure that nearly everything you do is helping you inch closer toward what's most important to you.

There is no such thing as an overnight success. Anyone who appears to be that has undoubtedly spent countless hours preparing themselves for the breakthrough moment. It's the work they've done behind closed doors, while others are resting, that has gotten them to their current place. Their success is the culmination of sacrifices, tiny details, and day after day of taking a step in the right direction. Big steps, small steps—it doesn't matter. If you commit to doing something, *anything*, that moves you closer to your goals every single day, you will get there eventually. It starts with having the discipline to do it when it's not fun, or when you want to take a break, or when there's something "better" going on. Often it requires you to do it even though you are unsure when or where the payoff will come.

Anyone can announce their intentions. Many people do. But no sooner than they make their declaration do they sit down on the couch and flip on the television. "Tomorrow" is setting up to be the most productive day in the history of the world. Everyone has that day marked on their calendar as the day that they are going to get started on their big plans. But the truth is, tomorrow never comes. It's only a day away and it's *always* a day away. "Today" is when it has to begin and it's got to continue, at least a little bit, for every new "today" that follows. Let everyone else wait for tomorrow if that's what they want to do, but *today* is your day to get to work. Today is the day to do what others won't.

#11
Have your cake, eat it, and don't apologize for your happiness.

You can have it all. You can have your cake and eat it, too. It's not up to anyone else to determine how happy you are allowed to be. The moment you start thinking that maybe you aren't deserving of something is the moment you start limiting yourself. You are deserving of all the good in life, just like anyone else. Being happy and having a life that is rich in the most important areas is something you should not only strive for, it's something you're entitled to. Happiness is free. It is created from within yourself and, as a result, there are no limits and no potential shortages. Our lives are meant to be happy and abundant. And no one can make it otherwise unless we let them.

There's this perception that a person who expects to have everything they desire is audacious. That it's not only impossible, but it's also greedy. The perception is wrong and close-minded. There is no reason to be ashamed for wanting the best that life has to offer. Are we supposed to limit ourselves? Is it possible to be too happy? Of course not. The person that thinks your expectations are too high, should consider raising their own instead. You will get exactly what you expect out of life. Nothing more, nothing less. It all comes from a choice you make. Your state of mind is entirely up to you. So, if you have the ability to choose what you want, why not choose to be happy? Why not choose to have the cake *and* a fork to go along with it?

The idea that you control your own happiness and that you can have as much as you choose to have is nice in theory, but how do you actually go about feeling that way every day? How do you ignore the hardships in your life to the point where you can still feel happy despite them? Those are fair questions, but the answer is really simple. You look for the silver lining. You remind yourself of the good that is still there. You just *decide* to be happy. Happy people aren't happy because everything in their life is terrific. It's not that they never get sick or sad or scared. It's just that when they start to notice those feelings they focus on health and joy and courage instead. They've decided that "happy" is going to be their state of normalcy, and anytime they feel themselves drifting from that state, they find a reason to return to happiness. There's always something to be happy about. And you usually don't even have to look that hard to find it.

When you decide to get the things you want out of life and to be a happy person, you will notice this way of thinking will come easier and easier for you the more you do it. That is because it's *natural* for us to be happy. It takes work to be—and remain—upset. But happiness and peacefulness comes naturally. As a result, you don't owe anyone an explanation for feeling that way. You don't have to feel ashamed, embarrassed or guilty that you're happy and someone else isn't. You're *supposed* to feel that way. You're *supposed* to enjoy your life. And you're *supposed* to share your happiness with others. Happiness is not something to shy away from. It's something to celebrate. And what's a celebration without some cake? I'll bring the forks.

#10

Roll your eyes all you want,
one day you'll sound just like your dad too.

I'm afraid it's true. No matter how hard you try, when you become a parent you will find yourself repeating many of the same things I say to you. One day you may suddenly stop and wonder how you could have gotten to that point. How could you have sunk so low as to tell your children exactly what you used to hate hearing from me? Well, I've got news for you. Just about all these lessons are thoughts or ideas that I was taught by *my* old man. They stuck with me, yes, because he taught them so frequently and feverishly that they were burned into my head, but also because I think they're pretty darn good lessons. And that's the part you have to understand. It's one thing to just repeat all that you were taught because that's what you heard, but it's a completely different thing to repeat all those things because that's what you *believe*.

You can read countless books and learn many great things, but unless you determine your own thoughts and come to your own conclusions, all you have is a collection of facts. It's not until you apply them to your own life in a way that makes sense to you, that their meaning becomes much more powerful and their impact much greater. It might be true that it was just some old man who came up with that idea hundreds of years ago—and the context could be completely different from now—but the message doesn't change much. The advice that carries down through generations has withstood the test of time, and though you may repeat what I say mostly out of familiarity, the value behind it is still there.

Even though you may hear about how this kind of thing happens—how children grow up to become their parents—it still is kind of funny when it happens to you. Then, before you've had barely a moment to smile, it quickly becomes terrifying. The pressure to set a good example and offer advice that builds character suddenly becomes very real. There is a future father and husband heeding my every word and mimicking my every action. As easily as I can shape you into a quality person if I do my job well, I can also ruin you if I do it poorly. And *that* is how the example of past generations can be helpful. It gives us something from which to build. They are the giants whose shoulders we stand upon.

My job is to build on what my dad has given me, and to give you the opportunity to build on who I've become. I can spend time teaching you right from wrong and explaining the ways of the world, but I've got to live that way myself. I've got to *show* you the way, in order to give you solid shoulders to stand upon. It's a daunting task—a challenge that goes beyond the general responsibilities of feeding and clothing you, which are needed to *sustain* life.

Once those basic needs are met, my job is then to *shape* life. When you think of it that way, it's easy to see the impact that can be made, good or bad. The advantage I have—as do many other dads—is the ability to "see" far and wide, thanks to my view from the shoulders of giants. My own dad has propped me up, and I intend to do the same for you so that, one day, you will be prepared to lift your own children.

#9
Anger does the most damage
to the one who possesses it. Let it go.

Let's say someone does you wrong. Maybe they lied to you, or harmed you physically. Maybe they took advantage of your loyalty. It would probably make you angry, as it would anyone else. Angry with them, angry with yourself for allowing it to happen. You might end up angry at the world because you don't know who or what else to blame. It's fine to feel anger. It lets you know that something's not right and alerts you to growing frustration. But in order to release the frustration, you have to process the anger first. You have to find a positive way to deal with it. Bottling it up inside can cause significant harm, and the longer you hang on to it, the more damage it does. When that damage occurs, it isn't done to the person you're upset with. You are the one who pays the price.

It takes effort to hold on to anger. Being mad is tiresome. It's much more taxing on your mind and body than being calm and relaxed. It wears on you, day by day, hour by hour, even when you're not directly thinking about it. Unless you work through it or let it go, it's still churning in the back of your mind. In the mean-time—though you may not realize—it's also holding you back. It prevents you from doing the things you should be doing to im-prove. It stands in the way of you receiving the good that is trying to come your way, and it blocks potential opportunities from pre-senting themselves. You focus so strongly on being mad that you ignore all the parts of life that should be making you happy. If this goes on long enough it will turn you cold, crass and bitter. And for what?

When we're angry we want the person who caused our anger to know that we're upset, and sometimes we want them to feel that same pain. *We were done wrong and someone needs to pay for it!* That kind of thinking might make us feel better at the time, but what good can possibly come of it? It's much more healthy and productive to work through it with that person in a constructive, civilized way. If they're not willing to hear you out, you *need* to find a way to let it go, even if you never get the apology or the recognition you feel you deserve. The offender probably moved on within moments of upsetting you, and when you fail to move on, you are making a bad situation even worse. You cannot control the actions of other peo-ple, but you *can* control how you react to what they do. So *choose* to not let their insensitivity, carelessness or cruelty cause you stress, anger or frustration. Learn what you can from it, and move on.

Life is much too short to spend any amount of time feeling angry. Understand that people are going to do things that upset you, accept that you will be disappointed from time to time, and then instead of focusing on the disappointment, find the cause. Determine how you can prevent it from happening again, and focus your energy on moving forward. Most importantly, forgive often. The toughest offenses to forgive are often the ones that you'll benefit from most. They are the biggest source of pain and stress, and they will lift the most weight off your chest. Swallow your pride when it's necessary to put your heart at ease. Anger does the most damage to the one who possesses it. Let it go.

#8

Ask questions; seek answers; absorb knowledge. Never stop learning.

There is always something new to be learned. There are discoveries to be made, mysteries to solve, and puzzles to piece together. No matter where your interests lie, or what your motivation may be, there is *always* more you can learn about a subject. If we spent every waking moment of our lives picking up new skills or ideas, we still wouldn't even get close to knowing all that there is to know. The information available to us is unlimited. That might seem overwhelming, but it's actually a good thing. Having so many questions keeps us interested in life and inspired to find answers. It allows us to go in whatever direction we choose, learning about whichever topic fascinates us, and it offers us a trip down the rabbit hole of information. And once you're down there, the possibilities are endless.

I think it helps if you look at learning like it's an adventure. It's a journey that should last your entire lifetime and should always be fun and exciting. Sometimes we form a bad opinion about learning because we base it on things we are forced to learn about in school. Not all subjects are going to be interesting to you, and some will be flat out boring. But it's important that you understand this difference: It's not learning that bores you, it's learning about things you're not interested in that is boring. Tough it out during those classes, knowing that your formal education is only a short portion of the time you're going to spend learning. Your education does not end upon graduation. If anything, that's when it really begins. At that point, you are free to spend your days and nights learning whatever it is that interests you. And you have a lifetime to do it.

The people who truly understand this lesson are the ones most familiar with the questions "why?" and "how?" They are not satisfied accepting an explanation like "that's just how things are." They want the details of the story. They want the mechanics of the operation. They want reasons *why* something is the way it is, and they want to know *how* it came to be that way. They are information sponges, absorbing as much knowledge as they can. And, as a result, they fuel progress, find breakthroughs and, perhaps most importantly, they feed their curiosity. We are not meant to be stagnant. By our nature, we want to develop and evolve and *improve*, but we can't do those things unless we commit to learning. When you stop learning, you stop growing.

Once you really commit to lifelong learning, one thing that will never be a problem for you again is boredom. There is simply no place for it in a world as fascinating as ours. There is too much to be amazed by or wonder about; there is too much to discover. Who has time to be bored? Not people who ask questions and seek answers. Certainly not people who have an insatiable appetite for absorbing knowledge. And definitely not someone committed to lifelong learning. You can take time to rest or reflect or sit idle, but when you find yourself contemplating how something works or why it is designed that way, act on it. Approach life with awe and wonder and curiosity, and accept nothing less than satisfactory answers to your questions. Take advantage of the information available at your fingertips. Most importantly, no matter what, never, ever, ever, *ever* stop learning.

#7

Advance confidently in
the direction of your dreams.

Confidence is the driving force behind just about all of our successes. Sure, things like ability, hard work and fortitude play a significant role as well, but without self-confidence we'd rarely have the courage to test our limits or dream big dreams. When you are sure of your abilities and trust your talents, then nothing is beyond your reach. A confident person knows that only they can stand in their own way. All other obstacles can and will be overcome. A confident person also believes in themselves, even when they cannot see the whole path before them. Confidence does not come from knowing *how* you are going to do something, but rather trusting that you *can* do it. It comes from having a staunch, unwavering belief that you are capable and that you will. It comes from believing that, with each new step you take, more of the path will appear.

Like most things, the more you practice putting confidence to work, the easier it will be to call on it in the future. It becomes a stronger, more reliable trait with each achievement, and it is there to pick you up again should you face defeat. If you nurture it, confidence will guide you through your darkest times and direct you toward the brightest of futures. You can do anything you dream, as long as you believe you can. You can be anyone you want, as long as you trust yourself. That doesn't mean there won't be periods of doubt, or times where you're afraid, or instances where you wonder if you'll fail, but these moments don't last in the mind of a confident person. A confident mind is not void of fear or doubt, but it quickly recognizes and removes them, making room for thoughts of progress and success.

The quickest way to turn confidence into progress and success is to visualize yourself excelling at those activities or fulfilling those dreams. Close your eyes and actually *see* yourself enjoying the satisfaction that success brings. Pay close attention to what it *feels* like to achieve your greatest desires. When you do this, you are preparing your mind and body to repeat it for real when you have the opportunity. You are training them for success. When two opponents of equal talent and desire meet, the edge often goes to the one with more experience. Through visualization, you are *experiencing* the road to victory. And once you've won in your mind, you will have no problem finding the confidence to do it again in the real world. You've been there before. You know what to do.

Yes, you can have whatever you want in life. It's true, you can do anything you decide and be anyone you choose. But if you are going to be that person and do those things, you need to believe it in your own mind first. You need to believe that the ability is within you, and you need to trust that your talents will shine through. I believe in you. I know you can do it. But unless *you* know it, it's unlikely to happen. So *know* it. Set the big goals. See yourself reaching them. And then walk, as the path reveals itself to you step by step, advancing confidently in the direction of your dreams.

#6

Life is short. Do what makes you happy.

We're not guaranteed tomorrow. We're not even guaranteed the rest of today. That's not a good enough reason to live recklessly, but it is *the* reason to live happily. We don't have enough time to mess around with things that we aren't enjoying. There's too much else we want to do—too many other things we *need* to do, instead. I've mentioned that there is a meaning to our lives—a purpose we're all supposed to fulfill—and when you are happy it means you are on track towards fulfilling it. Follow that feeling; enjoy life; live as though you're running out of time—because you are. We all are. I don't know about you, but I've got a lot I want to pack into the rest of my time here, and it starts with being happy, with not stressing about the minor worries. It starts with enjoying each day, each moment as if it were my last.

If you knew this were your last day or your last year, would you be living the way you are now? Would you be working the job you have now? Would you still be dating the person you're with? If the answer is "no" to any of those questions, then you've got some things to think about. If they aren't making you happy, if they're not right for you, then *why* are you still letting them take up so much of your time? Remember, time is all you have. It's an extremely limited resource and you can never make more of it, no matter how much money you have or how persuasive you are. So, if you're not happy with those parts of your life, improve them. Work on that relationship or scrap it. Find a way to like your current job better or find a new one. Discover your passion and then immerse yourself in it.

The simplest way to live happily is to make your passion your career. Find the one thing that, if money were no object, you would do without being paid. Then find a way to get paid for it. With just about every subject that exists, someone out there is already earning a living doing it. You *can* be happy to go to work. I bet you'd be hard pressed to find a movie critic that hated their job. And that's just one example. There are too many options and too many opportunities to allow yourself to be locked into the "security" of a job you hate. Stop wasting time doing what you don't want to do, and find a way to free yourself to do the things that make you smile, the things that make you feel like you're alive. It *is* possible. It *can* be done.

Life is short. Sometimes, life is *much* too short. We may say we *want* to be happy, and we may even think that we are, but then we're hit with some perspective and realize we aren't—not entirely at least. Maybe we're lying to ourselves. Maybe we're allowing someone else to define what makes us happy. Either way, it shouldn't take a tragedy to remind us that we aren't living fully. If anything, it should make us grateful that we *are*. You never know when the end might come, and when it does, what a shame it would be to have lived your life to someone else's standards. How sad it would be to have let yourself down. How unfortunate it would be to have left something on the table. Life is much too short to be anything but happy.

#5

Family is a constant. We'll never leave you, never steer you wrong.

People will come and go from your life. Some will stay longer and make a greater impact than others, but throughout the years things will change. Life changes. Relationships change. *You* will change. But one thing that will never change is your connection to family. We're here for the long haul—the good parts, the bad and everything in between. There may be times when you wish this isn't so, when you'll want us to just go away, but eventually you will realize that there is nothing else like the support of family—even when they're nosing through your business. You can't choose your family, but you also can't replicate the natural bond you have with them. Your family has a piece of you with them always, just as you carry them with you. It's a powerful source of strength and comfort.

Just because we'll always be there to support one another doesn't mean there won't be disagreements or conflict. In fact, the likelihood of problems increases *because* there is such a strong feeling of responsibility to each other. Families operate with an underlying layer of great passion and love, and sometimes those emotions overtake rational thought and self-control. Such passion has the potential to sometimes make things worse or blow them out of proportion, which is why it's important to remember that regardless of how it appears on the surface, the source is always unconditional love. Love is the most powerful emotion there is, and it often clouds judgment. Don't confuse someone who is intentionally trying to give you a hard time with someone who simply loves you and wants what's best for you.

Trust is among the most valuable benefits of being close with your family. Because you tend to spend more time with them than anyone else, and because you've known them your entire life, it becomes natural to trust them. When life gets rough and you find yourself in a difficult situation, knowing there are people you can trust will offer you peace of mind that you'll make it through. You can rely on them for support—whether it's emotional, financial or physical—and they will deliver the best they can, because that's what families do. In return, you must be someone that *they* can trust—someone *they* can count on to help when *they* are in need. It's important that you take this responsibility seriously, because not everyone is fortunate enough to have that support behind them.

Whether it be due to a falling out or estrangement or death, families do get broken up. In some cases, it's necessary for a person to look elsewhere for help. Although I don't intend for you to ever experience this with *your* family, sometimes things happen that are beyond our control. It is possible to develop that same bond with someone who isn't a relative. You don't have to share blood to be family. But you *do* have to share trust. And love. Whether it's someone you were born to, adopted by, or met three weeks ago, "family" is the people that guide you, that support you, that tell you the truth and hug you afterward. They don't follow their own agendas; they shoot you straight. They tell it like it is. They are there with you through all the peaks and valleys. In a world that changes by the moment, family is a constant. They'll never leave you, never steer you wrong.

#4

You may fall in and out of love with a woman or two, but *she* will always be your girl.

The "she" I'm referring to is your mom. The reality of romance is you'll likely have more relationships that *don't* work out than those that do. Women will come in and out of your life throughout the years. There will be puppy love, adolescent crushes, and teenage lust. There will be college girlfriends and casual dates and adult relationships. Then, one day, you will find the person that officially takes you off the market and you will live happily ever after. Or at least that's the idea. The same person could fill all those stages of "love" for you, but most likely as you grow you will meet different people and your circle of acquaintances will change with your experiences. But no matter where you are romantically, there will *always* be one woman whose heart you hold in the palm of your hand. That person is your mother. And that won't ever change.

There is a bond between a mother and her son that can't fairly be put into words. It's so complex and so deeply threaded throughout the soul that to try and explain it would be to do it a great injustice. It's an invisible connection of mutual love and respect. It's strong enough to resolve conflict and to create it. Still, as durable as it is, and as much as it's designed to last and to endure strain and wear and tear, it needs to be nurtured from time to time as well. You can't neglect the relationship you share with your mom unless you're willing to throw it away. She needs to know what she means to you, even as you begin to share your heart with another girl. There is enough love inside you to save some for your mom. So do it. Because she will always do the same for you.

One of the hardest things your mom will ever have to do is watch you fall in love. I can't imagine it would be easy for her to share that place in your heart. She will do it, because that's what loving mothers do, but it's going to take a special, special girl to get her to willingly give up that real estate. Choose that girl wisely. Make it an easy transition for your mom by finding someone that is so wonderful she'll know you'll be in good hands. The best thing for her, aside from being the lone love of your life, is to feel like the person she's making room for cares about you as much as she does. It's a peace of mind that all moms long for when their baby boys grow up.

If you make sure to keep a place for her—and to let her know often that it's there—when the day finally comes that you've found someone truly worthy, she'll be happy for you. No matter what happens, what your mom wants most is for you to be happy. Happiness and love. If you are able to get those two things out of life, then whether she's your only girl or if she's sharing your heart, she will be proud. From the moment she first felt you kick, you've held her heart in your hand. And that won't ever change. Although you may fall in and out of love with a woman or two, your mom will *always* be your girl.

#**3**

There will come a day when you'll wonder if you make me proud. You do...all the time.

I think every boy grows up with this thought on his mind. He will always try to live up to an image that his daddy will be proud of. It's not a bad thing, because it can inspire. A child can be motivated to meet those expectations and do great things as a result. But I think it can also cause them to be hard on themselves. It can create uncertainty, insecurity, or even a sadness that they will never become the man their dad wants them to be. It's a lot of pressure for a young person. And, most of the time, it's unnecessary. I'm telling you now—so there's never any doubt or concern—you make me proud. Every single day since the day you were born I've been proud to be your dad. I'm proud of the boy you are and I'm excited to see the man you become.

Just because I say you make me proud doesn't mean I expect you never to wonder about it. I know that's part of growing up and finding your way. Sometimes you'll second-guess yourself. You'll need reassurance that you're doing the right thing. And, in each of those cases, you'll think about how I would have wanted you to react. Maybe you'll be afraid you let me down. When this happens, remember one thing: As long as you always do what you believe to be right, you will make me proud.

There is no pressure to take over the family business. I have realistic expectations when it comes to my role in your life choices. You won't disappoint me if you don't follow in my footsteps. The pride I have in you doesn't come from the things you do as much as it comes from the person you are. When you start changing who you are to conform to expectations others have—even if that other person is me—you lose part of what makes you special. Your uniqueness and individuality is what I'm most proud of. You should be proud of it as well. Celebrate the fact that you are your own person. You are an extension of me thanks to blood and genetics—and hopefully due to values and ideals—but that is where it ends. Beyond that, *you* decide where you want this life to take you, and I won't stand in your way.

So the answer is *yes*. You *do* make me proud. Every minute of every day I am proud of you. I am humbled by the opportunity to be your dad, and as challenging as it may be at times, being a parent is the most rewarding thing there is in life. You might do *things* that disappoint me, but *you* will never disappoint me. Spend your time teaching and learning and loving rather than worrying about whether I'm proud or not. You could hit a million home runs or never even foul one off, and it won't change the way I feel about you. Keep *that* in your back pocket for those times when you're feeling down on yourself. When that day comes, and you begin to wonder again if you make me proud, remember what I'm saying to you now. *You do...all the time.*

#2
Never doubt how much you're loved.

Of all the possible things that can be questioned, whether or not you are loved should never be one of them. As parents, our children are the most precious things in our lives. They are the cause of our greatest joys as well as our most overwhelming frustrations, but no matter how high our low our moods swing, the deep-seated love doesn't budge. You are a blessing—an opinionated one, for sure, but a blessing nonetheless—and there is nothing you can do to change that fact. Things may not always be perfect, and from time to time the love will get buried beneath scolding and punishments, but just like on a rainy day, where the sun is always right behind the clouds, so too is our love for you. You may not always see it, you may not always feel it, but the love always there.

Loving someone unconditionally is easy and challenging at the same time. On one hand, the feeling runs so deeply that it can't be undone, regardless of what the person may say or do. Yet, on the other hand, it means standing by them in support and encouragement, even when they say or do something awful. You have that kind of love. And not just from your mom and me. It's all around you. In all honesty, it's all around everyone. They just have to acknowledge and embrace it, and be willing to offer it to others in return. It might seem sappy, and maybe even a little unrealistic, but how great would the world be if we all treated each other this way?

Sometimes it's easy to feel overlooked or forgotten about. Everyone gets preoccupied with their own lives from time to time, and it can make you feel like they don't care about you or what you might be going through. Don't confuse someone being distracted or busy with a lack of concern for you. You are loved by more people, and with more devotion, than you may ever realize. Even when you get the sense you are entirely on your own—or that no one really cares—there are people that love you and will have your back in a moment's notice. There is always someone you can turn to. You are never all alone, and you never will be.

In order for the love and support to be worthwhile, you have to be willing to accept it. Understand that the intention is always to create a situation that is best for you. Sometimes it works out and sometimes it doesn't, but that is always the goal. Don't push this love away. Allow us to be there for you because one day you'll realize you needed it more than you thought. It's a great feeling to be loved by someone, and an even better feeling to love them back in return. You have plenty of opportunity to experience both. Don't hesitate to share that emotion with those closest to you. Love them with all you have, and they will most certainly love you back. Only then—when you accept and share the love that surrounds you—might you be able to truly understand how much you are loved.

#1

One day, I'll be gone. You'll be okay; but if you need help, use these 100 things to remember my wish for you.

Everybody dies, bud. No matter what we try to do to prevent it, eventually our time will come. One day, *my* time will come. Sure, I hope it's not for many, many years, but these things aren't up to us. All *we* decide is how to spend the time we're given. Then, when our number is finally called, we hope we've lived well and left a legacy to be proud of. You kids will be my legacy, and I'm already proud of that.

Just because you know that I'm going to have to leave you one day doesn't mean it will be any easier for you to say goodbye. You will be sad. There will be things you miss about me—and probably some that you are happy to see go—but you will get through it. You will be okay. I'm confident of that, not because I know how strong you are (though I do), but because I know that you can always come back to these 100 things to hear my voice again. You can read my wishes for you anytime you want, and close the book when you've heard enough. I believe in each one of these lessons, or I wouldn't have written them. I hope that you will carefully consider their messages—weaving them into your own values—and that one day you'll teach them to your children, just as they were taught to me. Even if you disagree with most of what I've written, there is some of it that you must not ignore. The following values are mandates, not suggestions. Always live with them in mind.

Integrity. Your good word is the most important commitment you can make to someone. Be a person others can trust to do the right thing and to follow through on your promises. Be someone who is loyal and honest and genuine. Treat others the way all people deserve to be treated: with respect. Represent yourself and your family with class and dignity. *Be a good person.*

Create. Never, ever suppress your desire to create. Keep that spirit alive and nurture it so it always continues to grow and evolve. Learn as much as you possibly can and continue to do so for the rest of your life. Ask questions and seek their answers. Paint a picture, write a book, sing a song. Do *something* that makes you feel alive and allows you to explain the world from your perspective. *Be yourself.*

Live. Life is short, but meaningful. You are here for a reason. It's your responsibility to discover that purpose and make it come alive. Commit to reaching your potential and doing the very best you can. Spend your days living fully, getting the most out of life. Keep a positive attitude, a*lways*. Give of yourself and you will receive tenfold back. Be someone others want to be around. Feel emotions. Celebrate life. Stay healthy. Smile. Laugh. Cry. *Be happy.*

Dream. Always believe in yourself. You can do anything you want. Nothing is impossible. Stay confident that you can—and will—create the life you want to live. Dream big dreams and then turn them into reality. Ignore anyone who tells you otherwise. Don't let their self-limiting beliefs slow you down. Stare down fear. Defeat doubt. *Be a day dreamer.*

Love. It's the strongest thing in the world. Allow yourself to experience it. Share it with others. Open yourself up to romance. Search gently for your soul mate, and when you find her, don't ever let her go. Stand by your family; they love you without condition. Love them back. Just as love causes pain, it is also the reason for living. Treat it with the respect it deserves. *Be loving.*

Yes, after all those lessons, it really is mostly about these five things. The others are all important, but for the most part they fit here in some way. If you can make these values a major part of your life, keeping their concepts in the front of your mind and living accordingly, you can't lose.

Life is a mystery. No one truly knows what it's all about, but I have shared with you some of what I believe to be most important. I encourage you to consider them and then, ultimately, you will have to decide for yourself which pieces you want to buy into. I won't be here for all of it. I hope to be here for most, but one day I'll be gone. That's just how life goes. Let's spend our time knowing that day is going to come, and when it does, let's not wish we'd done anything differently. Let's get our hugs and kisses in whenever we have the chance. Let's throw that ball until it's too dark to see. Let's laugh together and make memories that outlast everything else. Even death.

In the meantime, I have a wish for you. It is that you will get everything you want in life. That you will find—and hold on to—happiness, and that your good days will far outnumber the bad. I wish you success in everything you do. I hope that you see all your wildest dreams become reality. And they will. As long as you believe.

Love always,

Dad

ABOUT THE AUTHOR

RJ Licata is the creator of LessonsandLove.com, where he writes about the rewards and challenges of raising children. Born and raised in Syracuse, NY, he currently lives in East Syracuse, NY with his wife, Danielle, and their two children, Joey and Gianna. They are expecting a third child in July. *Lessons for Joey* is his first book. Follow him on Twitter @RJLicata.

LESSONS & LOVE ONLINE

There are a few different ways to stay connected with Lessons & Love online. For the latest news and information on this book and future books be sure to follow us in the following places:

EMAIL NEWSLETTER – www.LessonsandLove.com/newsletter
Sign up to receive periodic updates about all things Lessons & Love. If you follow us in only one place, make this one it!

FACEBOOK – www.facebook.com/100ThingstoTeach
This is where it all started, and where we will continue to post exclusive content.

TWITTER – www.twitter.com/LessonsandLove
Insightful thoughts on life in 140 characters or less.

WEBSITE – www.LessonsandLove.com
The hub of the entire operation. Visit us on the web for good reads and more!